yOung Exceptional children

Monograph Series No. 10

Early Intervention for Infants and Toddlers and Their Families: Practices and Outcomes

**THE DIVISION FOR EARLY CHILDHOOD
OF THE COUNCIL FOR EXCEPTIONAL CHILDREN**

Carla A. Peterson, Lise Fox, and **Patricia M. Blasco**
Co-Editors

Disclaimer

The opinions and information contained in the articles in this publication are those of the authors of the respective articles and not necessarily those of the co-editors of the *Young Exceptional Children (YEC)* Monograph Series or of the Division for Early Childhood. Accordingly, the Division for Early Childhood assumes no liability or risk that may be incurred as a consequence, directly or indirectly, or the use and application of any of the contents of this publication.

The DEC does not perform due diligence on advertisers, exhibitors, or their products or services, and cannot endorse or guarantee that their offerings are suitable or accurate.

Division for Early Childhood (DEC) Executive Board

President Susan Maude
President-Elect Virginia Buysse
Vice-President Rosa Milagros Santos
Past-President Mark Innocenti
Secretary Kathy Hebbeler
Treasurer Rob Corroso
Governor Betsy Ayankoya
Members-At-Large Jim Lesko, Brian Boyd, Cindy Oser, Donna Dugger Wadsworth

DEC Standing Committee Chairs and Editors
Governmental Relations Committee Chair Bonnie Keilty
Membership Committee Chair Donna Nylander
Subdivision Committee Chair Billi L. Bromer
Personnel Preparation Committee Chair Judy Niemeyer
Research Committee Chair Dale Walker
Family Consortium Committee Chair Cheryl Rhodes
Multicultural Activities Committee Chair Hwa Lee
Publications Committee Chair Lise Fox
Partnership Committee Chair Rena Hallam
Information and Technology Committee Chair Ted Burke
Student Activities Committee Chair Judith Losh
Editor, *Journal of Early Intervention* William Brown
Editor, *Young Exceptional Children* Carla Peterson
Executive Director Sarah Mulligan
Governmental Relations Consultant Sharon Walsh
Director of Member Services Bethany Morris
Assistant to the Executive Director Cynthia Wood

Copyright 2008 by the Division for Early Childhood of the Council for Exceptional Children. All rights reserved. 09 08 07 06   2 3 4 5 6

No portion of this book may be reproduced by any means, electronic or otherwise, without the express written permission of the Division for Early Childhood.

ISSN 1096-2506 • ISBN 978-0-9773772-7-5

Printed in the United States of America

Published and Distributed by:

27 Fort Missoula Road, Suite 2
Missoula, MT 59804
(406) 543-0872
FAX (406) 543-0887
www.dec-sped.org

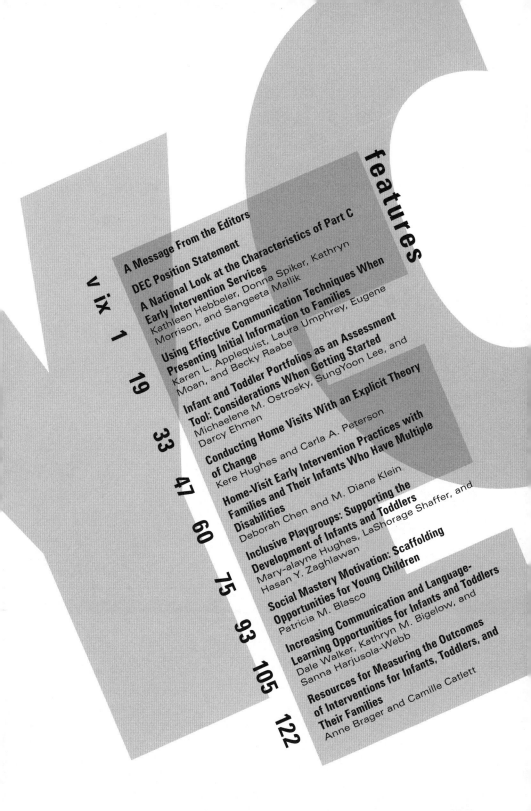

features

A Message From the Editors

Welcome to the tenth issue of the Young Exceptional Children Monograph Series highlighting infants, toddlers, and their families. This issue is devoted to articles designed to assist practitioners, family members, and students in understanding early intervention services as guided by recommended practices and enhanced by current knowledge of evidenced-based research and practices for young children and their families.

Early intervention services have been available throughout the country for more than 20 years; services are provided in a variety of settings and by individuals from a variety of disciplines. However, *DEC Recommended Practices in Early Intervention/Early Childhood Special Education* (Sandall, Hemmeter, Smith, & McLean, 2005) emphasize the importance of common features across these settings. These features are described in the articles presented here; as well, the importance of preparing professionals from a variety of disciplinary backgrounds to work with young children and their families will be illustrated. For example, the importance of family members and service providers building partnerships and the significant role that professionals play in establishing trusting relationships and using a culturally sensitive approach to establish respectful communications with family members are highlighted in several articles. As well, the importance of delivering intervention services in natural environments in order to maximize children's learning opportunities and the effectiveness of early intervention services is stressed. Additionally, we provide a reprint of DEC's position paper entitled "Prevention of Social, Emotional, Physical, and Cognitive Disabilities and the Promotion of Health, Safety and Well-Being." We encourage you to copy this statement and share it with your colleagues.

The first article by Hebbeler and her colleagues provides an overview of early intervention services across the country. These authors, reporting information from the National Early Intervention Longitudinal Study (NEILS), describe the range of early intervention services provided to children and families, the professionals who provide those services, and the settings in which children and families participate. These descriptions help readers understand both the common elements of services that many families receive and the great variability in services from family to family. Also, this article highlights some of the challenges that remain as we strive to make early intervention services as effective as possible.

Families almost always enter early intervention services because of concerns regarding their child's developmental status—often after their child has been evaluated by a variety of professionals and possibly given a medical diagnosis of some kind. Most families feel very vulnerable at this point, and practitioners often find it necessary to deliver information regarding disappointing evaluation results and poor developmental progress. Applequist and her colleagues offer very practical ideas that will help practitioners provide families appropriate supports while still communicating with them clearly.

Effective intervention is dependent upon accurate, timely, and useful assessment information. Ostrosky and her colleagues present creative suggestions that will help practitioners maximize the use of assessment portfolios with infants and toddlers. Portfolios are more often used with preschool-aged children in classroom programs; this article highlights ways that portfolios can be used successfully with younger children, how families can contribute to their child's portfolio, and how the portfolio can be used to document and guide interventions.

The next two articles provide guidance to maximize the effectiveness of home visiting interventions. The NEILS data remind us that most families participating in early intervention receive at least some of those services through home visits; unfortunately, many practitioners have received very little training regarding home visiting services in their preservice programs. Hughes and Peterson discuss the importance of engaging both parents and children in home visiting activities, explaining the purposes of activities, and providing coaching support and reinforcement as parents try new interaction strategies. Using triadic interaction strategies sets the stage for parents to develop the competence and confidence needed to help them maximize their children's learning opportunities as well as enhance their enjoyment of their child. Together, these strategies serve to make explicit the theory of change guiding home visiting interventions. Chen and Klein expand the discussion of home visiting interventions by providing practical strategies to use when working with families parenting children who have multiple disabilities.

Hughes and her colleagues describe using strategies similar to those suggested for use during home visits in another setting. The setting, inclusive play groups, is different, but the goals are similar. These authors provide suggestions for strategies that interventionists can use to facilitate parent-child interactions designed to enhance parents' understanding of their child's development, the importance of their roles in scaffolding learning, and their own enjoyment of interacting with their child.

The final two articles turn our focus to strategies that interventionists and families can use to enhance their children's development in specific areas. Blasco highlights the importance of recognizing and supporting children's social mastery motivation and provides several vignettes to illustrate strategies that can be used to do this. Walker and her colleagues detail strategies that can be used, across settings and by various adults, to increase young children's language-learning opportunities and enhance their communication skills.

The final feature of this tenth monograph is a "Resources Within Reason" column prepared by Anne Brager and Camille Catlett. They have followed the pattern established in each issue of *Young Exceptional Children* by providing information regarding a variety of materials and information sources that will be useful for measuring the outcomes of interventions for infants, toddlers, and their families.

Contributing Reviewers

Harriet Able Boone, University of North Carolina at Chapel Hill
Becky Adelman, Oregon Health Sciences University
David Allen, Portland State University
Ann Bingham, University of Nevada-Reno
Virginia Buyssee, University of North Carolina at Chapel Hill
Deborah Chen, California State University, Northridge
Nitasha Clark, Vanderbilt University
Shelley Clarke, University of South Florida
Laurie Dinnebeil, University of Toledo
Paddy Favazza, Rhode Island College
Janice Fialka, Early On Training and Technical Assistance (Part C), Huntington Woods, MI
Ann Garfinkle, University of Montana-Missoula
Marci Hanson, San Francisco State University
Cheryl Hitchcock, Tennessee Technological University
Kere Hughes, Iowa State University
LeeAnn Jung, University of Kentucky
Cecile Komara, University of Alabama
Marisa Macy, Pennsylvania State University
Chris Marvin, University of Nebraska-Lincoln
Rebecca McCathren, University of Missouri
Andrea Morris, University of Illinois
Leslie Munson, Portland State University
Lisa Naig, Iowa State University
Missy Olive, Center for Autism and Related Disorders, Austin, TX
Diane Powell, University of South Florida
Beth Rous, University of Kentucky
Susan Sandall, University of Washington
Tamara Sewell, Adelphi University
Patricia Snyder, University of Florida
Vicki Turbiville, Dripping Springs, TX
Bobbie Vaughn, University of South Florida
Dale Walker, University of Kansas

Reference

Sandall, S., Hemmeter, M. L., Smith, B. S., & McLean, M. (2005). *DEC recommended practices: A comprehensive guide*. Longmont, CO: Sopris West.

Co-Editors: Carla A. Peterson (carlapet@iastate.edu)
Lise Fox (fox@fhmi.usf.edu)
Patricia M. Blasco (blascop@ohsu.edu)

Coming Next!

The topic for the 11th *Young Exceptional Children*
Monograph is "Quality Inclusive Services in a Diverse
Society." For more information, check the announce-
ments section of *Young Exceptional Children* (Volume 12,
Number 1) or go to **http:/www.dec-sped.org**.

POSITION STATEMENT

ADOPTED: APRIL 2000

Prevention of Social, Emotional, Physical and Cognitive Disabilities and the Promotion of Health, Safety and Well-Being

The Division for Early Childhood (DEC) of the Council for Exceptional Children supports local, state, and federal initiatives to promote the health, safety, and well-being and the prevention of social, physical and cognitive disabilities including efforts taken to assure that children affected by disabilities do not acquire unnecessary secondary disabilities or exacerbation of their impairments.

Research has shown that the early childhood years build the foundation for a lifetime of health and development. Well-known factors have also shown that investing in prevention is cost-effective and that services need to be provided in natural environments with collaborative efforts to establish linkages with appropriate community-based systems, services and personnel.

Resources to address the biological and environmental components of risk factors for young children may include:

1. Prenatal care services for all pregnant women and their families;

2. Early and periodic screening, diagnosis, and treatment, including well-child checks and safe vaccinations provided to all children who should receive these services as established in the concept of the medical home*;

3. Culturally responsive family and parenting education and support programs for families with risk factors (e.g., teenagers and other individuals at high risk);

4. Early intervention programs and other programs aimed at reduction of social and environmental factors related to risk conditions in early childhood (e.g., abuse/neglect, substance abuse, poverty, lead poisoning, violence) and at enhancing the child's capacity to negotiate those environments; and

5. Affordable, quality childcare environments ensuring that young children are in safe, healthy, nurturing environments that provide high quality early experiences to promote development and learning.

Therefore, DEC supports the advancement of programs, policies and practices supported through evidenced-based practice and empirical research. DEC believes that there should be substantial attention and resources devoted to prevention and intervention, including:

1. Research to develop and evaluate educational, behavioral, medical, and environmental interventions during the prenatal period aimed at buffering or ameliorating disabling conditions;

2. Practices that are developmentally and individually appropriate, family-centered and inclusive (vital to preventing or reducing the severity of many disabilities or at-risk conditions and prevent secondary conditions);

3. Service systems that are culturally responsive, family-centered, and coordinated across all states, provinces, and territories provided by qualified, credentialed professionals and paraprofessionals;

4. Support for families as decision-makers in partnership with professionals with regard to the health and well-being of their children;

5. Advocacy for informed, research-based, fully funded, and effectively implemented public regulations and policies aimed at services for young children with special needs that are provided in safe, healthy, and nurturing learning environments; and

Division for Early Childhood
27 Fort Missoula Road • Missoula, MT 59804 • Phone: 406.543.0872 • Fax: 406.543.0887
E-mail: dec@dec-sped.org • www.dec-sped.org

PERMISSION TO COPY NOT REQUIRED – DISTRIBUTION ENCOURAGED   PAGE 1 OF 2

POSITION STATEMENT: Prevention of Social, Emotional, Physical and Cognitive Disabilities and the Promotion of Health, Safety and Well-Being

6. Dissemination of information that promotes the translation and transference of evidenced-based knowledge and empirically based research information to practice, resulting in higher-quality services for children and families.

*A medical home is not a building, house, or hospital, but rather an approach to providing healthcare services in a high-quality and cost-effective manner. (American Academy of Pediatric, from www.medicalhomeinfo.org).

RESOURCES

American Academy of Pediatrics. (2005, November). Policy statement: Care coordination in the medical home: Integrating health and related systems of care for children with special health care needs. *Pediatrics, 116*(5), 1238-1244.

American Academy of Pediatrics. (2001, July). Policy Statement: Developmental Surveillance and Screening of Infants and Young Children. Pediatrics, *108*(1), 192-195.

Association for Retarded Citizens and American Association on Mental Retardation. (2002, November). *Position statement: Early intervention.* Retrieved March 4, 2006, from http://www.thearc.org/posits/earlyintpos.doc

National Association for the Education of Young Children. (1996). Prevention of child abuse in early childhood programs and the responsibilities of early childhood professionals to prevent child abuse. Retrieved March 4, 2006, from http://www.naeyc.org/about/positions/pschab98.asp

Sandall, S., McLean, M.E., & Smith, B.J. (2000). DEC recommended practices in early intervention/Early Childhood Special Education. Longmont, CO: Sopris West.

Zero to Three Policy Center (2004, May 18). Promoting Healthy Social and Emotional Development. Retrieved March 4, 2006, from http://www.zerotothree.org/policy/factsheets/IMHstate.pdf

APPROVED BY DEC EXECUTIVE BOARD: APRIL 7, 2006
REAFFIRMED BY DEC EXECUTIVE BOARD: AUGUST 21, 2007

Division for Early Childhood
27 Fort Missoula Road • Missoula, MT 59804 • Phone: 406.543.0872 • Fax: 406.543.0887
E-mail: dec@dec-sped.org • www.dec-sped.org

A National Look at the Characteristics of Part C Early Intervention Services

Kathleen Hebbeler, Ph.D.

Donna Spiker, Ph.D.

Kathryn Morrison, MSPT

Sangeeta Mallik, Ph.D.
SRI International, Menlo Park, CA

Early intervention, as provided under Part C of the Individuals With Disabilities Education Act (IDEA), encompasses a variety of programs and services aimed at the prevention and remediation of developmental difficulties, delays, and disorders in children from birth to 36 months of age (Guralnick, 2005a; Spiker & Hebbeler, 1999). The services provided by early intervention programs should be individualized to the needs of the child and the family and thus will vary with regard to the type, location, and quantity of service provided. Early intervention services are provided by professionals and paraprofessionals from a variety of disciplines, including persons with training in early childhood special education, developmental and clinical psychology, speech pathology and communication disorders, physical and occupational therapy, child psychiatry, social work, nursing, and other fields. The services are delivered in several types of locations such as children's homes, doctor's offices or clinics, specialized early intervention centers, and preschools.

Part C of IDEA specifies the basic minimum components of an early intervention system but provides states discretion in determining the exact population to be served and in structuring the service delivery system (Gallagher, Harbin, Eckland, & Clifford, 1994; Garwood & Sheehan, 1989; Johnson et al., 1994). Given the flexibility states are allowed, it is not surprising that early intervention services vary considerably from state to state with regard to facets of service delivery such as who is served, what agencies provide services, and how providing agencies coordinate with other agencies in the community (Spiker, Hebbeler, Wagner, Cameto, & McKenna, 2000). The federal law identifies 16 services that are to be provided through early intervention programs (Table 1); however, these services are provided through different public or private agencies in different states (Spiker et al.).

The National Early Intervention Longitudinal Study (NEILS) followed a nationally representative sample of children and families receiving early intervention and collected data on the characteristics of early intervention recipients, the services they received, and the outcomes they achieved. The NEILS dataset provides the most comprehensive information available about the early intervention services received by young children and their families. As the NEILS findings demonstrate, it is challenging to characterize what constitutes typical early intervention services. Using data from the NEILS, this paper presents descriptive information about the characteristics of early intervention services provided to children and their families in the United States.

Table 1
Early Intervention Services in IDEA

Assistive technology
Audiology
Family training, counseling, and home visits
Health services
Medical services only for diagnostic or evaluation purposes
Nursing services
Nutrition services
Occupational therapy
Physical therapy
Psychological services
Service coordination services
Social work services
Special instruction
Speech-language pathology
Transportation and related costs
Vision services

Note. IDEA = Individuals With Disabilities Education Act.

How Were NEILS Data Collected?

The NEILS followed a nationally representative sample of 3,338 children (birth to age 3) and their families, from their entry into early intervention until kindergarten. The families began early intervention services for the first time between September 1997 and November 1998. Families were recruited through early intervention programs located in 93 counties in 20 states. Local program providers explained the study to families at or near the time the initial individualized family service plan (IFSP) was developed. All families who met the study criteria (child less than 31 months of age and an adult in the household who spoke English or Spanish) were invited to participate. Programs invited 4,653 families to participate in the study and 3,338 (72%) agreed. The NEILS provides the most comprehensive information available about the early intervention services received by young children and their families.

When each child entered the study, the enrolling program was asked to identify the "most knowledgeable provider" for the child, someone who could provide the requested information about the services provided. This provider was mailed a questionnaire, called a Service Record, every 6 months for as long as the child remained in early intervention. The information shared here is based on the first Service Record sent to early intervention service providers, which represents approximately the first 6 months of the family's services.

Characteristics of Early Intervention Services

More research on early intervention is needed to identify which characteristics of services are most important for producing good outcomes for young children and their families. Nevertheless, IDEA, as well as recommended practice, stresses the importance of some features of early intervention services. For example, the language of IDEA strongly encourages that services be provided in the "natural environment," such as the home and community settings where children without disabilities spend their time. The legislation also recognizes the importance of qualified providers. Determining what constitutes optimal early intervention services is complicated by the distinct possibility that it may not be a single characteristic of services but the combination of several that leads to the best outcomes for any individual child and family. Given the number of characteristics of early intervention services, many such combinations are possible.

This paper presents information on seven characteristics of early intervention services: (1) setting, (2) number and types of services, (3) types of providers, (4) amount of services scheduled and missed, (5) focus of services, (6) number of other children participating in services, and (7) consultation among providers.

Setting

Providers were asked to record where the child had received services in the previous 6 months. Options included the family's home, a family child care or preschool/nursery school setting, a specialized center-based early intervention program, a clinic or office (e.g., hospital-based clinic or therapist's office), or another setting (e.g., inpatient services in a hospital). Home was by far the most frequent setting, with almost 8 out of every 10 children and families receiving services in this setting during their first 6 months of services (Figure 1). Almost 3 in 10 received services in centers and in clinics and nearly 1 in 10 received services in preschool or child care settings.

The majority of children and families received services in only one setting (57%); however, one third received services in two settings (33%), and nearly 1 in 10 received services in three or more settings (8%). Several combinations of service settings were identified. The most common setting was a single setting: 41% of children and families were scheduled to

Figure 1
Percentage of Children and Families Who Received Early Intervention Services in Each Setting (n = 2,820)

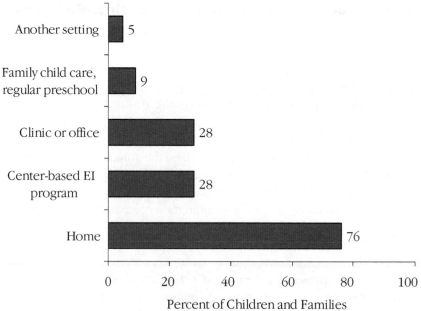

Percent of Children and Families

Figure 2
Combinations of Settings in Which Children and Families Received Services (*n* = 2,739)

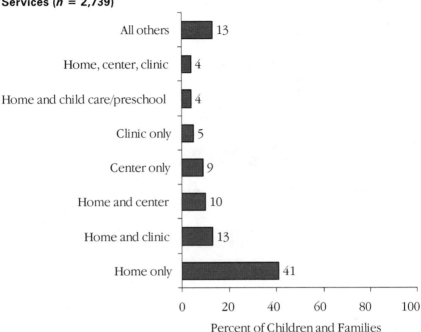

Percent of Children and Families

receive services only in the home (Figure 2). All other single or multiple setting combinations applied to far fewer children and families.

Number and Types of Services

IDEA identifies 16 different types of early intervention services, but the findings from the NEILS show that in practice, 6 services make up the core of early intervention. Each of the core 6 services was received by more than one third of the children (Figure 3); a much smaller percentage of children and families received the other services. The service most frequently provided to children and families during their first 6 months in early intervention was service coordination, with almost 8 out of every 10 children and families reported as having received this service. Because IDEA requires that service coordination be offered to all children and families receiving early intervention, it is somewhat surprising that the percentage was less than 100. It is possible that some families declined service coordination or chose to serve as their own service coordinators or that some service providers failed to report that the child and family were receiving service coordination.

The next most frequently provided service was speech/language therapy, which was provided to slightly more than half of the children (52%).

Figure 3
Percentage of Children and Families Who Received the Most Frequently Provided Early Intervention Services (*n* = 2,820)

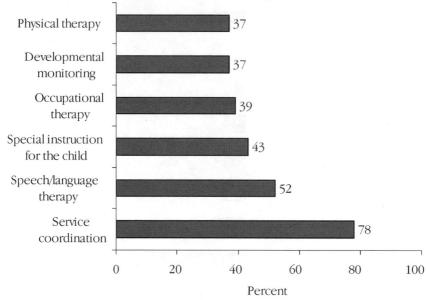

Other services frequently provided were special instruction, occupational therapy, developmental monitoring, and physical therapy; each was provided to about 4 of every 10 children. All other early intervention services, including family training, social work, nutrition services, and nursing services, among others, were received by fewer than one in five children. Specialized, health-related, and diagnostic services such as genetic counseling, mental health counseling, and assistive technology were provided to less than 5% of children and families.

Providers indicated that during their first 6 months in early intervention, 28% of children and families received two or fewer different types of early intervention services, and 72% received three or more types (Figure 4). About one fourth of children and families received six or more services. A very small percentage of families (3%) were reported to have received no services in the first 6 months after they had enrolled in early intervention.

Types of Providers
The professionals who provide early intervention services, not surprisingly, parallel the types of services most frequently provided. During the first 6 months in early intervention, nearly two thirds (63%) of families were reported to have worked with a service coordinator (Figure 5).

Figure 4
Number of Services Scheduled in the First 6 Months of Early Intervention
(n = 2,820)

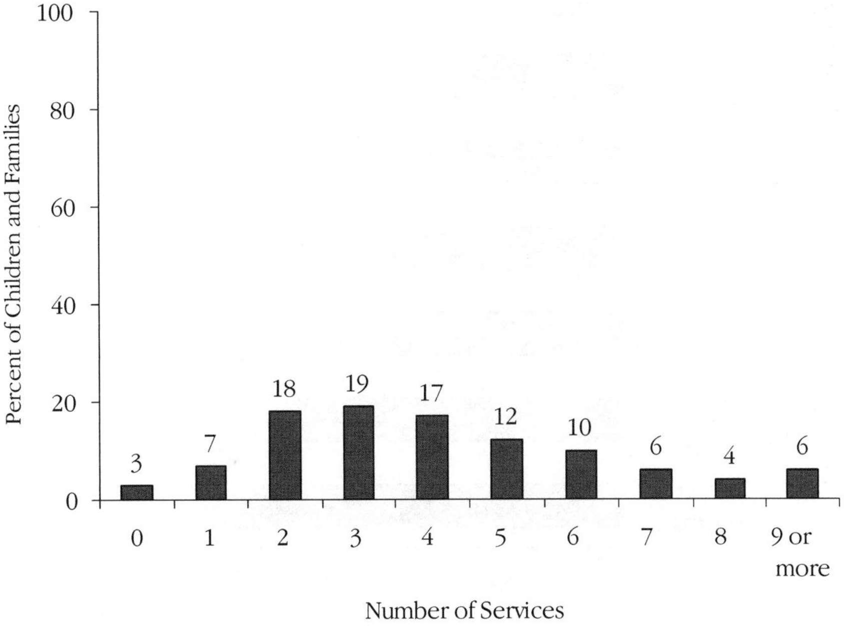

Number of Services

This percentage is even less than the 78% who were reported to have received service coordination, but the lower number could be a reflection of the way in which the information was collected. The form used to collect these data, the Service Record, was organized around settings (e.g., home, center) with a series of questions asked about each setting. One of these questions asked the respondent to mark each of the professionals who provided services in that setting. Service coordination might not be delivered in one of these settings in the way that a therapy or child development service is delivered. Rather, activities related to service coordination might take place over the phone or in an office. Also, another professional such as a physical therapist might fill the role of the service coordinator, but the respondent could have mistakenly indicated only one role rather than two for this professional.

More than half (53%) of the families worked with a speech therapist. Other common providers were occupational therapists and physical therapists (38% of families worked with each), child development specialists (32%), and special educators (29%). The child development/infant specialist and the special educator appear to play a similar role labeled with a different title depending on locality and perhaps the type of educational or training background, because almost no families worked with both

Figure 5
Percentage of Children and Families Served by Early Intervention Professionals (Includes Only Professionals Who Worked With 28% or More Families) (_n_ = 2,803)

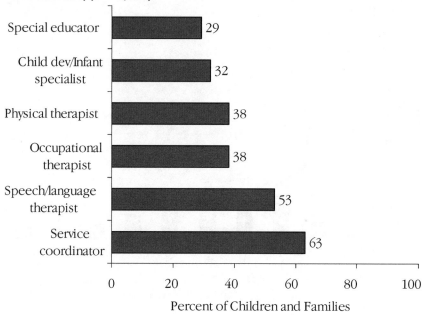

Percent of Children and Families

of these professionals. Similar to the findings on types of services, there were many other professionals who worked with only a small percentage of families.

The median number of providers for families during their first 6 months in early intervention was 3, with an average of 3.3. The number of providers ranged from 0 to 13 with nearly one fourth of families having had 5 or more providers (Figure 6). A small percentage of families had no providers because they did not receive any services after the development of the IFSP.

Amount of Service Scheduled and Missed

The amount of service scheduled for families is a potentially important factor, because it may relate to the impact of the services on the child and family, and it has direct cost implications for programs. Much remains to be learned about the relationship between amount of services and outcomes achieved (National Research Council and Institute of Medicine, 2000). There may well be an ideal threshold range below which early intervention cannot be effective but above which services intrude on families without adding significant impact on the child's development and level of functioning. Too many hours of service could mean substantial

Figure 6
Number of Different Types of Service Providers Working with a Child or Family (*n* = 2,803)

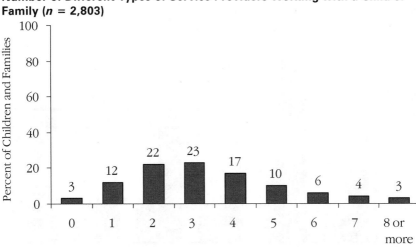

Number of Different Service Provider Types

portions of a week devoted to early intervention and could negatively impact a family's ability to go about everyday routines.

The amount of service scheduled to be provided over the course of the first 6 months in early intervention was collected for each setting in which the child and family was to receive services and then was summed across settings to produce a total amount of service. All data were converted to minutes of service per week. In each setting, the mean is substantially larger than the median, which reflects the fact that some children were scheduled to receive far more service than others; this raised the overall average. Given this, the median may be the more meaningful number, because it reflects most closely the amount of services that most children were receiving.

The amount of service to be provided varied substantially by setting (Figure 7). Across all settings, the median amount of service scheduled to be provided each week was 1.5 hours. In the home, the setting where three out of four families received services, the median amount of scheduled service was 1 hour per week. In specialized centers, a setting where about one in four families received services, the median amount was 1.8 hours per week. About one in four also received services in a clinic or office, and the median amount for this setting was 0.6 hour per week. For services in child care settings and in other settings, the median scheduled amounts were 1 hour and .5 hours, respectively, per week.

As noted previously, the difference between the mean and the median indicates variation in the amount of services different families received.

Figure 7
Mean and Median Amount of Scheduled Service per Week by Setting
(*n* = 2,697)

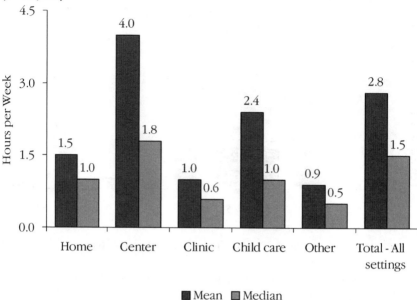

■ Mean ■ Median

This variation showed a different pattern across settings. One fourth of the families who received services in the home were scheduled for 30 minutes or less per week, and 83% were scheduled for 2 hours or less. At the other end of the spectrum, 5% of the families were scheduled to receive more than 4 hours of service per week in their homes. The variation seen in the amount of services scheduled in center-based programs most likely reflects variation in program models. Most families (59%) were scheduled to receive services for 2 hours per week or less in a center. This amount of service could indicate a model where the parent brought the child to a therapist or for a type of special intervention. Slightly more than one fourth of families (27%), however, were scheduled to receive more than 4 hours of services per week in a center. The program for these families could have been group services, such as a preschool, which the child attended several mornings a week.

Less variation was found in the amount of scheduled clinic-based services. The largest proportion of families (47%) was scheduled to receive 30 minutes or less of services per week in a clinic. Another 38% were scheduled for between 31 minutes and 2 hours. These findings could reflect service patterns in which services were provided less than weekly. For example, some of the children shown as receiving less than 30 minutes per week could have been receiving 50 minutes every other week.

The percentage distribution of total amount of service per week shows that most families were scheduled to receive 2 hours or less of service per week, with the most common amount being 1 to 2 hours per week (Figure 8). At the extremes, 13% of the families were scheduled for 30 minutes or less per week and 9% were scheduled for more than 6 hours per week.

The data presented address the amount of service that children and families were scheduled to receive. Many families, however, do not receive all scheduled services. Respondents were asked to provide the percentage of scheduled service within each setting that the child and family had missed in the preceding 6 months. Because the amount of missing data on this item was unusually high (data were not provided for 36% of children and families) the information on amount of service missed should be interpreted cautiously.

Overall, providers reported that, on average, families missed 23% of their scheduled services. Given that the median amount of scheduled service was 1.5 hours per week, this would mean the typical family in early intervention received a little over an hour per week of service during their first 6 months of early intervention. There was some variation across settings in amount of service missed (Figure 9), with the highest average percentage of services missed found for specialized centers.

Figure 8
Total Amount of Services Scheduled across All Settings (*n* = 2,697)

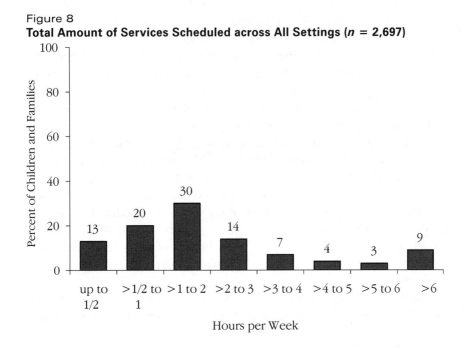

Figure 9
Provider Estimate of the Amount of Service Missed by Children and Families in the Previous 6 Months by Setting (*n* = 2,020)

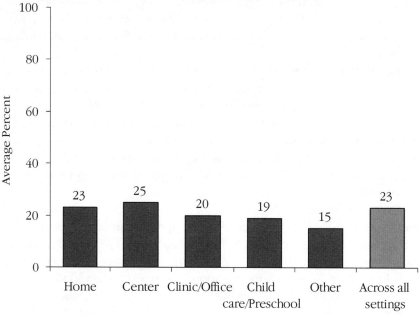

Although the average amount of services missed in the home was 23%, this amount varied considerably across families. Nearly one fourth of children and families (22%) were reported to have missed no services in the first 6 months of early intervention, and another 15% were reported to have missed 10% or less. Providers reported almost 1 in 10 families (8%) to have missed more than 50% of their home-based services. The numbers for center-based services are slightly different: 17% of families were reported to have missed none of their center-based services, and another 16% missed 10% or less. Similar to home-based services, a small percentage of families missed a great deal of service: 11% of families missed more than 50% of their center-based services. Although the average amount of service missed in clinics was only slightly less than the average for home- or center-based services, the distribution of amount of services missed was very different. Almost a third of the families scheduled to receive services in clinics were reported to have never missed those services (30%), and 6% of families missed 10% or less of their services. Again, some families missed a lot of services, with 8% reported to have missed more than 50%.

There are numerous reasons why families do not receive all of the services they are scheduled to receive. Providers reported that most families missed services for reasons related to the child, for example, because the child was ill (71% of families). The second most common reason for missing services was for reasons related to the family, such as not being able to keep an appointment (57%), and the third most common reason was related to the provider (33%).

Focus of Service

To obtain additional information about how services were delivered, providers were asked to indicate whether the primary focus of service was the child, the parent or guardian, or both the child and the adult. For more than half of the families (55%), services provided in the home were focused on both the child and the adult, and for another 44%, services were focused mainly on the child. Almost no families received services in the home that were focused mainly on the adult (<1%).

Number of Other Children Participating in Service

For services provided in a specialized center, a clinic, a preschool or child care, and other settings, the service provider was asked to indicate whether services were provided individually or in groups. Families and children who received services in specialized centers received services in various configurations (Figure 10). More than one third of children and families (35%) went to a specialized center for services that were provided only one-to-one, and another 20% received services that were mostly one-to-one. More than a third (36%) received services that were delivered mainly in groups, with the remainder (9%) receiving services only in groups. This is consistent with the data presented earlier on amount of service received in this setting, with some children going to the center for a therapy service and others going for longer amounts of time and spending time with other children.

Clinic services were overwhelmingly delivered individually, with 96% of those who received services in a clinic receiving one-to-one services. Services in preschools and child care centers were more varied but were still most likely to have been provided individually: About half (52%) of the services delivered were one-to-one, and another 22% were mainly one-to-one (Figure 10). This suggests a model where the therapist or provider was going to the preschool to provide the service. About a quarter (26%) of children and families served in preschools received services that were either mostly or exclusively group services. Services delivered in "other" settings, which applied to 5% of children and families, were provided predominantly on an individual basis.

Figure 10
Individual or Group Services by Setting (*n* = 110–775)

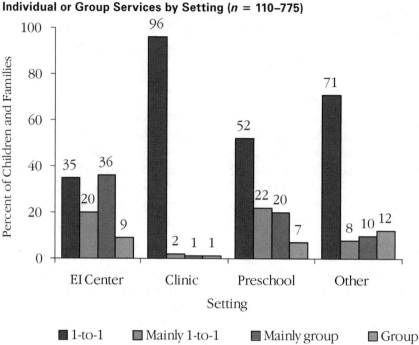

Consultation Among Providers

In a transdisciplinary model of service provision, providers are encouraged to work together to serve a family (Bruder, 2000, 2005; Guralnick, 2005b). A single provider working directly with the family would work collaboratively with other professionals who share their expertise, and thus the family would not need to work individually with a cadre of therapists. There are also many professionals whose expertise might be needed occasionally but not consistently for a child or family, and this professional could be consulted as needed. The providers were given a list of early intervention professionals and asked to check all who had consulted with other professionals about the child or family in the previous 6 months.

A variety of professionals were identified as having consulted about the child or family, although the most frequently consulted providers were the same professionals who provided the most direct service to families. For 69% of the families, the service coordinator was involved in consultation. Also, speech/language therapists (50%), occupational therapists (39%), and physical therapists (36%) were consulted frequently.

Conclusions

The NEILS findings present a complex and interesting picture of early intervention services. IDEA identifies a number of different services that could be provided to children who have developmental delays, established conditions, and risk conditions and to their families. Because services are to be individualized to the needs of each child and family, it would not be surprising to find considerable variation in what constitutes early intervention. The data presented here substantiate that early intervention does indeed take different forms for different children and families, but the findings also show some common themes across the features examined. The data indicate that although a variety of services are being provided through the early intervention system, the services most commonly provided are special instruction or child development services, speech therapy, occupational therapy, physical therapy, developmental monitoring, and service coordination. The NEILS data also show that the typical child in early intervention receives two to four services, services are most often provided in the home, and the typical family is working with providers from three different disciplines.

Combining the data on amount of service scheduled with the data on amount of service missed suggests that the typical family participates in early intervention services for a little over an hour per week, similar to data reported by other researchers (Harbin, McWilliam, & Gallagher, 2000; Hauser-Cram, Warfield, Shonkoff, & Krauss, 2001). This relatively small amount of service is especially noteworthy given that most families are working with more than one provider. Much remains to be learned about how much early intervention should be provided, and furthermore, the answer to the question is almost certainly different for children and families with different kinds of needs. Nevertheless, this small amount of service being provided for many families, especially if it is divided across different kinds of providers, raises questions about whether more services would lead to greater impact for children and families.

Amount of service is only one dimension of service, and it may not be the most important one. Given the highly interpersonal nature of early intervention, the quality of the relationship between the provider and the child and family and the nature of the activities that take place during their interactions are almost certainly more critical to the impact of early intervention on the child and family. Because NEILS used large-scale survey methodology, it was not well suited to collect data on these qualitative dimensions of service delivery.

The study did provide information regarding the focus of services and the number of other children present in settings outside the home.

Services in the home, the setting where most families received their services, were reported to be mainly focused on the child for 44% of children and families and to be focused on both the adult and child for another 55%. The high percentage of services reported to be focused primarily on the child was somewhat surprising. Services focused on adults, on helping the parents learn to work with their children, have the potential to lead to a greater impact on children, given the number of hours that caregivers spend with children compared with the limited amount of time an early intervention professional spends (Dunst & Bruder, 2002; Dunst, Bruder, Trivette, & Hamby, 2006). Focusing on the adult and child and helping the parent to recognize all of the many learning opportunities that exist in the child's daily life and family and community routines are consistent with recommended practice (Bruder, 2000; Bruder & Dunst, 1999; Dunst & Bruder; Spiker, Hebbeler, & Mallik, 2005). More research is needed to learn why providers are not routinely incorporating family training into their intervention plans. The high percentage of child-focused service combined with the relatively small amount of service being delivered suggests that the potential effectiveness of early intervention services could be increased by using that time to help parents acquire techniques to work with their children.

Inferences from the NEILS data are somewhat limited because the study could not address the more qualitative dimensions of early intervention service delivery. Also, the data were collected in 1998 and 1999, and it is possible that the emphasis on natural environments in the intervening years and other ongoing developments in the early intervention field have reduced the proportion of children receiving services in specialized centers or clinics. Other changes such as changes in professional development or funding policies also may have impacted how services are provided since these data were collected. Nevertheless, these are the only nationally representative data describing the provision of early intervention services.

The variety of services being provided along with the differences across families in what services they received suggests that early intervention is an individualized system of services. The findings underscore the complexity of the enterprise we call early intervention and suggest areas meriting further study, especially the amount of service families are receiving, why families are missing services, and why providers are delivering services focused on the child. More studies like NEILS are needed to examine how early intervention is provided, not just what it should be or could be. Researchers need to look at the quality of early intervention, especially with regard to how professionals are interacting with parents in early intervention and what they are trying to accomplish. In particular, are interventionists working to support parents so that they can provide the child with optimal learning opportunities throughout the day (i.e., how best to turn a few hours of service into many hours of early intervention for the child)? Overall, what modifications to early intervention systems should be put in place to ensure that more effective practices are implemented nationwide? The NEILS findings provide considerable information about early intervention services, but much remains to be learned about how to combine the various characteristics of early intervention services into service packages that will be highly individualized and at the same time produce the greatest impact on children and families.

Box 1
More information about NEILS is available

See www.sri.com/neils for reports and additional information about NEILS, including a copy of the Service Record.

Additional information about the sampling strategy is available in Javitz, H., Spiker, D., Hebbeler, K., & Wagner, M. (2002). *National Early Intervention Longitudinal Study: Sampling and weighting procedures: Enrollment form, family interview, service records* (NEILS Methodology Report No. 1). Menlo Park, CA: SRI International.

Characteristics of children and families who receive services are described in other reports: Hebbeler, K., Spiker, D., Bailey, D., Scarborough, A., Mallik, S., Simeonsson, R., et al. (2007). *Early intervention for infants and toddlers with disabilities and their families: Participants, services, and outcomes. Final report of the National Early Intervention Longitudinal Study (NEILS)*. Menlo Park, CA: SRI International.

Scarborough, A. A., Hebbeler, K. M., & Spiker, D. (2006). Eligibility characteristics of infants and toddlers entering early intervention in the United States. *Journal of Policy and Practice in Intellectual Disabilities, 3*(1), 57-64.

Scarborough, A. A., Spiker, D., Mallik, S., Hebbeler, K. M., Bailey, D. B., Jr., & Simeonsson, R. J. (2004). A national look at children and families entering early intervention. *Exceptional Children, 70*(4), 469-483.

Note
This study was conducted with support from the U.S. Department Education, Office of Special Education Programs (H159E50001) and the Institute for Education Sciences (R423A070064).

The authors wish to thank the families who participated in the study and the professionals who worked with them and provided the information reported in this paper.

You may contact Kathleen Hebbeler by email at kathleen.hebbeler@sri.com

References
Bruder, M. B. (2000). Family-centered early intervention: Clarifying our values for the new millennium. *Topics in Early Childhood Special Education, 20*(2), 105-115, 122.

Bruder, M. B. (2005). Service coordination and integration in a developmental systems approach to early intervention. In M. J. Guralnick (Ed.), *The developmental systems approach to early intervention* (pp. 29-58). Baltimore: Brookes.

Bruder, M. B. & Dunst, C. J. (1999). Expanding learning opportunities for infants and toddlers in natural environments: A chance to reconceptualize early intervention. *Zero to Three, 20,* 34-36.

Dunst, C. J. & Bruder, M. B. (2002). Valued outcomes of service coordination, early intervention, and natural environments. *Exceptional Children, 68,* 361-375.

Dunst, C. J., Bruder, M. B., Trivette, C. M., & Hamby, D. W. (2006). Everyday activity settings, natural learning environments, and early intervention practices. *Journal of Policy and Practice in Intellectual Disabilities, 3*(1), 3-10.

Gallagher, J. J., Harbin, G. L., Eckland, J., & Clifford, R. (1994). State diversity and policy implementation: Infants and toddlers. In L. J. Johnson, R. J. Gallagher, M. J. LaMontagne, J. B. Jordan, J. J. Gallagher, P. L. Hutinger, et al. (Eds.), *Meeting early intervention challenges: Issues from birth to three* (2nd ed., pp. 235-250). Baltimore: Brookes.

Garwood, S. G. & Sheehan, R. (1989). *Designing a comprehensive early intervention system: The challenge of Public Law 99-457.* Austin, TX: PRO-ED.

Guralnick, M. J. (Ed.). (2005a). *The developmental systems approach to early intervention.* Baltimore: Brookes.

Guralnick, M. J. (2005b). An overview of the developmental systems model for early intervention. In M. J. Guralnick (Ed.), *The developmental systems approach to early intervention* (pp. 3-28). Baltimore: Brookes.

Harbin, G. L., McWilliam, R. A., & Gallagher, J. J. (2000). Services for young children with disabilities and their families. In J. P. Shonkoff & S. J. Meisels (Eds.), *Handbook of early childhood intervention* (2nd ed., pp. 387-415). New York: Cambridge University Press.

Hauser-Cram, P., Warfield, M. E., Shonkoff, J. P., & Krauss, M. W. (2001). Children with disabilities: A longitudinal study of child development and parent well-being. *Monographs of the Society for Research in Child Development, 66*(3).

Johnson, L. J., Gallagher, R. J., LaMontagne, M. J., Jordan, J. B., Gallagher, J. J., Hutinger, P. L., et al. (Eds.). (1994). *Meeting early intervention challenges: Issues from birth to three.* Baltimore: Brookes.

National Research Council and Institute of Medicine. (2000). *From neurons to neighborhoods: The science of early childhood development.* Washington, DC: National Academy Press.

Spiker, D. & Hebbeler, K. (1999). Early intervention services. In M. Levine, W. B. Carey, & A. C. Crocker (Eds.), *Developmental-behavioral pediatrics* (3rd ed., pp. 793-802). Philadelphia: Saunders.

Spiker, D., Hebbeler, K., & Mallik, S. (2005). Developing and implementing early intervention programs for children with established disabilities. In M. J. Guralnick (Ed.), *The developmental systems approach to early intervention* (pp. 305-349). Baltimore: Brookes.

Spiker, D., Hebbeler, K., Wagner, M., Cameto, R., & McKenna, P. (2000). A framework for describing variations in state early intervention systems. *Topics in Early Childhood Special Education, 20*(4), 195-207.

Using Effective Communication Techniques When Presenting Initial Information to Families

Karen L. Applequist, Ph.D.

Laura Umphrey, Ph.D.

Eugene Moan, Ed.D.

Becky Raabe, M.A.
Northern Arizona University

Emilio and Maria Montoya suspected something was wrong when Angelica's development continued to lag several months behind that of her twin brother, Arturo. At age 20 months, Angelica could not walk independently, in stark contrast to Arturo, who was running and climbing. The Montoyas reluctantly discussed their concerns with the pediatrician, who recommended a developmental evaluation. He suggested they call the Developmental Clinic soon to schedule the evaluation.

The Montoyas arrived at the busy Developmental Clinic a few minutes before their appointment. The registration form was passed through a narrow receptionist's window. The application was perplexing; unfamiliar terminology and the disclosing of personal information caused them to momentarily reconsider the necessity of Angelica's evaluation.

Emilio and Maria's anxiety escalated as they carried their two children down the hallway to meet Dr. Smith, a developmental psychologist; Ms. Johnson, a physical therapist; and Ms. Grunig, a speech and language pathologist. They each introduced themselves to the family, briefly described the evaluation process, and proceeded with a standardized interview that all families complete. The professionals then turned their attention to Angelica's evaluation. Even though the Montoyas could communicate in English, they exchanged questioning looks as they tried to understand the purpose of the various tests. Mr. Montoya did his best to keep Arturo occupied; however, he eventually took the toddler to the waiting room. Maria was relieved *when the session ended. Dr. Smith asked that she join her husband in the waiting room and return to his office in 20 minutes to discuss the results.*

When they returned to Dr. Smith's office, they took seats across the room from the professionals. The solemn expression of each of the professionals alarmed Angelica's parents. They soon learned why— Dr. Smith abruptly disclosed the results of the evaluation and shattered the Montoya's hopes that Angelica would develop typically like her brother, Arturo. They were stunned. They didn't know how to respond or what questions to ask. The professionals continued with a lengthy explanation of their evaluation results. They received a referral for early intervention services and a list of service agencies and family support groups, none of which related to the family's Hispanic culture. The Montoyas couldn't comprehend realistic expectations for Angelica's future. They left the office feeling overwhelmed and helpless.

Life is unexpectedly transformed for parents when they learn their child has a disability. Starting with the disclosure of their child's diagnosis, parents confront personal grief and question the significance of the disability. They feel pressured to make immediate decisions about their child's care and are worried about their child's future. Likewise, they may be concerned about the effect their child's disability will have on their relationship and family. This is only the beginning of a unique parenting process that relies heavily on their relationship with professionals and access to information and support (Smith, 2003). Early intervention professionals can provide information about the child's disability, the services and support available, and any educational considerations. However, initial experiences for some families often take place in a clinical or hospital setting. These experiences influence the family's expectations for future collaborations with professionals.

Yet professionals seldom find the presentation of initial evaluation information an easy undertaking. Most professional organizations have established guidelines and broad recommendations pertaining to family-centered practice (e.g., American Academy of Pediatrics, 2003; Sandall, Hemmeter, Smith, & McLean, 2005), and many early-intervention professionals are trained in the principles of family-centered practices. Even though communication is recognized as integral to family-centered practice (Blue-Banning, Summers, Frankland, Nelson, & Beegle, 2004), it often does not receive sufficient emphasis in training curricula (Rupiper & Marvin, 2004). Professionals, therefore, may be inadequately prepared to use effective communication strategies (Brown, Stewart, & Ryan, 2003). This article presents recommendations and strategies for communicating initial evaluation information to families based on the communication literature. These guidelines center on setting the stage contextually, preparing for the exchange, and tailoring messages that are appropriate for use in a variety of settings.

Communicating Initial Evaluation Information to Families

Setting the Stage: Contextual Issues

Elements of the physical environment can have an influence on how people communicate (duPre, 2000). Parents of children with disabilities emphasized the importance of receiving information in contexts they consider safe (Mitchell & Sloper, 2002). Consequently, whenever possible, information should be shared in a setting in which the family is comfortable. While it may be helpful to arrange the furniture in some settings to eliminate artificial barriers and encourage greater intimacy, it is equally important that professionals respect the personal space of others.

Consider all elements of the location, including seating, room temperature, air quality, and the presence of visual or auditory stimuli (Williams, 1997). Professionals who routinely meet with families in clinical settings should consider ways to welcome families and make them feel comfortable. Meeting with families in non-clinical settings of the family's choosing is always preferable. When meeting with families in their home, distracting noise such as a loud television or interruptions by children may occur. Professionals will have to determine whether these negatively impact anyone's ability to participate actively in the meeting. Tolerance of distractions is highly variable, making it necessary to monitor the family's response patterns as well as your own. Sensitivity to different smells may cause discomfort in a family and should be eliminated if possible. This may mean choosing not to wear perfume that could be objectionable.

Allocating sufficient time for the information exchange results in a greater likelihood that families will have the opportunity to seek clarification and ask follow-up questions (Larsen & Smith, 1981). To do this the professional must give the family his or her undivided attention, uninterrupted by cell phones or a preoccupation with time. Americans rigidly adhere to set schedules and times, while those from different cultural communities may not (Hall, 1976; Lynch & Hanson, 2004). Recognize how your beliefs and behaviors about time impact your interactions with families.

Vignette Revisited: How It Should Be. The clinic modified registration procedures to diminish the Montoya's uncertainty about the evaluation. Forms were revised to be linguistically and culturally sensitive to families, and the use of unfamiliar terminology was eliminated. To reach out to families whose primary language is not English, forms were translated into Spanish. Interpreters were made available to families that needed them. Center staff scheduled a sufficient amount of time to offer assistance to complete the application, explain the evaluation process, and encourage Angelica's parents to ask questions. The initial interaction eased Emilio and Maria's anxiety. Dr. Smith warmly greeted Mr. and Mrs. Montoya and led them to his office. Angelica and Arturo were occupied with toys not too far away from the comfortable seating area where their parents and the professionals exchanged introductions and discussed the evaluation procedures. Dr. Smith explained why it was necessary for a physical therapist and speech language pathologist to also evaluate Angelica and provided an overview of what to expect.

Preparation

The preliminary step, and perhaps the most crucial one, is to fine-tune one's ability to be genuinely family centered. To do this, professionals must first reflect on their own beliefs, attitudes, and biases, as these will influence their ability to communicate with families. An individual's experiences and beliefs about disability will impact his or her expectations regarding the child's potential and interactions with families. Self-reflection can yield important insights into personal feelings about some families that may interfere with the ability to be responsive and sensitive to their unique strengths and needs. This is particularly true of families who are culturally or linguistically diverse, as professionals may embrace beliefs derived from stereotypes or limited understandings of different cultures. Self-reflection does not occur as a discrete step; rather, it should be occurring continuously as team members interact with families. Moreover, using an approach such as one described by Barrera and Corso (2002), referred to as a "skilled dialogue" (p. 103), in which professionals seek greater understanding of each family's unique beliefs and practices, is highly recommended as it eliminates stereotypical generalizations. Professionals who use this approach resist embracing assumptions about families; instead, they allow the family to share their values and beliefs freely. Dr. Jones may have assumed the Montoyas would defer to the professionals as experts and decide to only share essential information. If he were using the skilled dialogue approach, he would allow more time to explore their concerns and needs and be more responsive to their unique beliefs, resources, and priorities.

Families and professionals work together toward shared goals that address informational and emotional needs of the family. Families place high priority on obtaining information about developmental expectations, their child's developmental evaluation results, and ways to help their child (Bailey & Powell, 2005). The initial interaction with families sets the stage for all subsequent interactions and, therefore, should be carefully planned. Prior to the meeting, families should be encouraged to think about questions, consider who they would like to be present, and bring a pen and paper for taking notes.

Introductions

An important component of all exchanges is the introduction. Family anxiety is normally heightened in initial interactions because of concerns about diagnoses and evaluation results, medical expenses, or procedural ambiguity; therefore, it is important that the professional set the stage for the interaction with the family. Introductions involve establishing rapport and orienting the family (Stewart & Cash, 2008). At this time it is important that the professional introduce herself and explain her role. Keep in mind that although the professional may have gone through this process on numerous occasions with many families, it is new to each family and they are unfamiliar with the team members and their respective roles. Thus, the goal of rapport building is to establish and sustain a relationship with the family by creating feelings of goodwill and trust (Stewart & Cash, 2008). The second part of the introduction is the orienting phase. Orienting the family involves telling the family the purpose, length, and nature of the interview (Stewart & Cash, 2008). By the end of the introduction, the family knows what to expect during the visit, and both uncertainty and ambiguity are reduced.

In the first meeting with a family, it is important to set the stage so that parents are comfortable taking an active role in all interactions. Some families may see the professional as the person with all of the knowledge and expertise and the parent's role as one of listening to and receiving information. Therefore, it is important for the professional to ask for feedback, since most families will not interrupt (du Pre, 2000). Another strategy to encourage openness is verbal encouragement (du Pre, 2000). Techniques for facilitating verbal encouragement include using open-ended questions, not rushing the family or trying to fill silence, and avoiding abrupt topic shifts (if you need to change the topic, do so by telling the family, "Thank you for sharing, now I would like to ask you a few questions about..."). By doing this, the professional avoids appearing as though she or he is not listening (Smith & Hoppe, 1991). Families may have multiple concerns regarding their child. It is important to follow up with probing questions such as, "Is there anything else you would like to discuss today?" (Stewart & Cash, 2008). Also, duPre (2000) suggested that beyond a diagnosis and follow-up care, individuals seek to be "reassured, forgiven, comforted . . . ." Words mean a lot ("You needn't feel embarrassed about this," "It's not your fault").

When sharing evaluation information with a family or explaining a diagnosed condition or label, it is important to encourage family members to discuss how they perceive that information. Questions such as "What, if anything, have you heard about _____ ?" or "Have you any experiences with _____?" can be helpful.

Professionals may lack sufficient training to work effectively with families who are in stress. McCubbin (1983) presented the ABCX model that describes stressors, events, a person's available resources for addressing the stressors, and the outcomes. Asking the family how they have coped with challenges in the past can help the family focus on their coping abilities and resources. Professionals can be more empathic and strategic if they have this background information. While it is important to understand a family's unique styles of coping, Turnbull, Turbiville, and Turnbull (2000) recommend an empowerment model when working with families. The role of the professional, in this model, is to be responsive to the family by allowing them to identify their own goals and needs. The family retains control over their own lives, and professionals offer information and support the family needs to reach their goals.

Some research suggests that professionals may (unconsciously) engage in blocking behaviors that steer a conversation with a family away from complaints and emotional disclosures (Jarrett & Payne, 1995). It is important for the professional to be aware of this tendency and to actively try to create an open environment that facilitates family disclosure of concerns. Many families will not automatically feel comfortable in taking the lead in advocating on behalf of their child and family. It is the responsibility of the professional to give parents the opportunity to participate at the level of their choosing.

Vignette Revisited: How It Should Be. The time the professionals took preparing the Montoyas for the evaluation resulted in a parent-professional relationship based on trust and respect. Emilio and Maria returned a week after the evaluation with formulated questions, confident team members had listened carefully to their concerns about Angelica and conducted a thorough evaluation. The already established rapport, coupled with the psychologist's skill to compassionately deliver a diagnosis of life-long disability, lessened the shock of hearing Angelica had special needs. Ms. Johnson, the physical therapist, and Mrs. Grunig, the speech language pathologist, were also present to review the results of their evaluations and answer any questions the Montoyas had.

Tailoring Messages

Though families historically have expressed a desire for information about their child's needs and the types of services available (Gowen, Schoen, & Sparling, 1993), each family has its own unique needs for information. Therefore, the professional should respond to those needs by tailoring his or her approach to the individual family. Professionals using approaches such as the Family-Focused Interview (Winton, 1988) or the Routines-Based Interview (McWilliam, 1992) will often find that specific informational needs will be revealed during the course of the interview. The importance of listening to families is vital so that the possibility of offering information that is incomplete or creating "information overload" does not occur.

It is essential that professionals abandon personal agendas and adopt an approach that is responsive to the family at any given time. While professionals may decide the family needs further information regarding the child's diagnosis, the family may not be ready for that information. If they are not ready, then they may be less accepting of what is offered.

Part C of IDEA requires evaluations to be conducted in the family's native language, necessitating the use of interpreters for families who are not fluent in English. When communicating with a family through an interpreter, always speak directly to the family and not to the interpreter. When communicating with families whose primary language is not English, it is recommended that a vocabulary easier for them to understand is used. In fact, whenever possible avoid using vocabulary or professional jargon any family may have difficulty comprehending. The cultural dissonance some families experience may be alleviated by having a cultural mentor present.

Verbal Communication of Professionals

Families entering early intervention services are quickly submersed in a sea of acronyms and technical jargon. Acronyms are often used to communicate more efficiently but are useful only if everyone involved understands their meaning. Assuming the same definitions of common terminology can result in ineffective communication (Hadlow & Pitts,

1991). Therefore, it is important to make sure that the professional and the family have shared meanings for what may seem to be common terms. It may be helpful to say "When I use this term _____ , it can mean different things to different people. Here's what I mean by it . . . ."

Professionals should communicate with all family members present, giving them time to absorb what has been said before proceeding, particularly if they are struggling emotionally with the information. Pausing frequently will give parents time to process the information and the opportunity to ask questions. Professionals may not allow families to respond or offer comments and fail to tailor their messages, offering more information than is needed or desired (Brady, Peters, Gamel-McCormick, & Venuto, 2004).

On average, we remember only a fraction of what we hear (Ley, 1988). Because families are experiencing a high volume of new information and fluctuating emotions during the first years of their child's life, they may remember very little of what they hear in any particular meeting. Therefore, it may be necessary to repeat information often and offer it through other formats (e.g., written materials or web-based sources). It can be helpful to summarize what was presented in each individual exchange. Reviewing what was discussed at subsequent meetings gives the family the opportunity to hear it more than once. It may be helpful to summarize what was said in writing for the family to review later. Reassure or remind families that they might not absorb all the information shared during this first session. This will normalize a common worry for families and reduce feelings of guilt for not being able to absorb all of the information in one sitting.

Nonverbal Communication of Professionals

The nonverbal behavior of a professional can influence the outcome of an interaction with a family (Robinson, 1998; Roter, Frankel, Hall, & Sluyter, 2006). When we communicate to others we use different nonverbal behaviors that are typically classified as codes (DiMatteo, Hays, & Prince, 1986). These include vocalics (pitch, loudness, sighs, and laughter), kinesics (body movement, gaze, facial expression, and posture), proxemics (the use of space and territory), chronemics (how time is scheduled and structured), artifacts (the use of objects and environmental features to communicate), and haptics (touch). For communication to be most effective, nonverbal and verbal communication should be synchronous.

Beginning at birth, humans are able to communicate their emotions through facial expressions. While most of these are universal, some cultural variations occur. Because families who are in emotional turmoil will likely reveal their feelings nonverbally, professionals must learn to read their cues and respond accordingly (Pendleton, Schofield, Tate, & Havelock, 1984). One's face and body should reflect genuine interest to the family (Bensing, Kerssens, & van der Pasch, 1995). To encourage family participation, nonverbal affiliative cues should be used (Street & Buller, 1987).

For some the use of touch when communicating emotionally laden information might be consoling, while for others it may be culturally inappropriate. It is recommended that touch be used only if the professional can gauge that it will be accepted by family members (Northouse & Northouse, 1985).

While listening, it is important to provide nonverbal affiliative cues such as smiling, nodding, eye contact, and forward lean (O'Hair, Friedrich, & Dixon, 2007; Romig, 1996). Effective listening communicates approachability and trust (Romig, 1996). When listening to families, it is important to understand not only what they are saying but also to evaluate why they are saying it and to understand their feelings (Wright, Sparks, & O'Hair, 2008). People have reported that "the feeling of being understood is intrinsically therapeutic" (Suchman, Markakis, Beckman, & Frankel, 1997, p. 678). As a result of effective listening, families will communicate more freely when they feel a professional is genuinely listening (Bensing, Kerssens, & van der Pasch, 1995).

Vignette Revisited: How It Should Be. All of the team members skillfully responded to the Montoya's verbal and nonverbal reactions to the diagnosis. They allowed time for the family to absorb the results of each evaluation. They gauged the type and amount of information Emilio and Maria needed to understand Angelica's diagnosis; however, they didn't assume the information was understandable or sufficient. Toward the end of the meeting, Dr. Smith summarized the information presented so that the family would benefit from hearing it more than once. The professionals encouraged Angelica's parents to ask questions and asked a cultural mentor to be present. They discussed early intervention options, expectations, and potential outcomes. The family was asked if they would like to have information in different formats, and some materials were made available to them. Emilio and Maria were reassured by the team's sincere concern for Angelica. They left feeling hopeful.

Conclusion

As professionals we frequently emphasize technical expertise over information sharing. If we understand those strategies that promote more

Table 1
Checklist for Sharing Information

1. Did you allow time to develop rapport with the family and orient them?
2. Did you minimize the likelihood of making assumptions about the family and their willingness and ability to express themselves?
3. Did you select a setting that the family desired for your meeting?
4. Did you make an effort to minimize distractions during the meeting?
5. Was sufficient time allowed for the meeting so that it wasn't rushed?
6. Was the family encouraged to identify their informational needs?
7. Was the information shared accurate and bias free?
8. Was an interpreter present if needed?
9. Were you able to communicate using minimal jargon or acronyms?
10. Did you monitor the family's understanding of the information present and make necessary adjustments?
11. Was your verbal and nonverbal communication in synchrony?
12. Was information conveyed so that everyone could easily understand it?
13. Did you communicate to all family members?
14. Was sufficient time allowed for the family to process the information and ask questions?
15. Was the family given the opportunity to hear important information more than once?
16. Were Web site addresses and other materials presented if the family requested them?

effective communication of information to families, we can fulfill our roles more completely. Table 1 presents a checklist of questions the authors developed for professionals, and additional resources pertaining to this topic are included in Table 2. Many factors influence whether families get the information they need when they need it. For example, most families can now access information readily on the Internet, and many families may prefer to do so. Suggesting certain Web sites that present accurate and complete information may be helpful to these families. The volume of information available to families on the Internet can be overwhelming (Hart & Wyatt, 2004), so it is important to offer other sources of information including brochures, pamphlets, and multimedia materials to families who desire that. Resist making assumptions that all families

Table 2
Selected Resources

Books
Barerra, I., Corso, R. M., & Macpherson, D. (2003). *Skilled dialogue: Strategies for responding to cultural diversity in early childhood*. Baltimore: Paul H. Brookes Publishing. This book presents a model of cultural competence. The first two sections of the book describe the challenges professionals face in building relationships with culturally diverse families and the skilled dialogue model. In the third section specific approaches are presented.
Hanson, M. J. & Lynch, E. W. (2004). *Understanding families: Approaches to diversity, disability and risk*. Baltimore: Paul H. Brookes Publishing. This book is divided into three sections, beginning with a description of family diversity and its impact on families who have children with disabilities. Factors influencing risk and prevention are discussed in the next section. Approaches are highlighted in the third section that includes a chapter focused on communicating with families.
Buckman, M. D. (1992). *How to break bad news: A guide for health care professionals*. Baltimore: Johns Hopkins University Press. This book is designed for health care professionals who routinely present sensitive diagnostic information to individuals and families.

Video
Chen, D., Chan, S., & Brekken, L. (Producers). (1999). *Conversations for Three*. Videotape. Available from Brookes Publishing, Baltimore, MD. This videotape and accompanying discussion book present recommended practices for working with interpreters.

Articles and Pamphlets
Educational Resources Information Center. (1991). *Communicating with culturally diverse parents of exceptional children* (Report No. E497). Reston: VA. (ERIC Document Reproduction Service No. ED333619). A copy of this article is on the Vanderbilt University, IRIS Center Web site: http://iris.peabody.vanderbilt.edu/info_briefs/eric/ericdigests/ed333619.pdf
Pamphlet: *Help your patients succeed: Tips for Communication*. http://www.clearhealthcommunication.org/pdf/help-your-patients.pdf
Mueller, P. S. (2002). Breaking bad news to patients: The SPIKES approach can make this difficult task easier. http://www.postgradmed.com/issues/2002/09_02/editorial_sep.htm

Table 2 (*continued*)
Selected Resources

Web sites
The Beach Center on Disability includes information and resources on many topics. http://www.beachcenter.org
The Institute for Family-Centered Care includes resources for health professionals. http://www.familycenteredcare.org/
The National Center for Cultural Competence sponsored by Georgetown University Center for Child and Human Development includes an extensive collection for professionals and families on cultural competence. http://www11.georgetown.edu/research/gucchd/nccc/
Partnership for Clear Health Communication at the National Patient Foundation. http://www.healthierus.gov/steps/2006Slides/C3/boles.html
Web site includes information for health care professionals:
http://www.askme3.org/
http://www.pacer.org/publications/earlyChildhood.asp. The PACER Web site offers publications useful for partnering with families.
http://clas.uiuc.edu/ The home page for Culturally and Linguistically Appropriate Services: Early Childhood Research Institute includes many publications focused on developing relationships with diverse families

want information in all of these different formats and ask them about their preferences. Information about parent-to-parent or family-to-family resources and supports should be given to families. It is the responsibility of professionals to recognize these factors that influence how families receive information and to modify their approaches so that families can become informed decision makers.

References

American Academy of Pediatrics. (2003). Family-centered care and the pediatrician's role. *Pediatrics, 112,* 691-696.

Bailey, D. B. & Powell, T. (2005). Assessing the information needs of families in early intervention. In M.J. Guralnick (Ed.), *The developmental systems approach to early intervention* (pp. 151-184). Baltimore: Paul H. Brookes Publishing.

Barrera, I. & Corso, R. (2002). Cultural competence: A skilled dialogue. *Topics in Early Childhood Special Education, 22,* 103-113.

Bensing, J. M., Kerssens, J. J., & van der Pasch, M. (1995). Patient-directed gaze as a tool for discovering and handling psychosocial problems in general practice. *Journal of Nonverbal Behavior, 19,* 223-242.

Blue-Banning, M., Summers, J. A., Frankland, H. C., Nelson, L. L., & Beegle, G. (2004). Dimensions of family and professional partnerships: Constructive guidelines for collaboration. *Exceptional Children, 70,* 167-185.

Brady, S., Peters, D., Gamel-McCormick, M., & Venuto, N. (2004). Types and patterns of professional-family talk in home-based early intervention. *Journal of Early Intervention, 26*(2), 146-159.

Brown, J. B., Stewart, M., & Ryan, B. L. (2003). Outcomes of patient-provider interaction. In T. L. Thompson, A. M. Dorsey, K. I. Miller & R. Parrot (Eds.), *Handbook of health communication*. Mahwah, NJ: Lawrence Erlbaum Associates.

Chaitchik, S., Kreitler, S., Shaked, S., Schwartz I., & Rosin, R. (1992). Doctor-patient communication in a cancer ward. *Journal of Cancer Education, 7,* 41-46.

DiMatteo, M. R., Hays, R. D., & Prince, L. M. (1986). Relationship of physicians' nonverbal communication skill to patient satisfaction, appointment noncompliance, and physician workload. *Health Psychology, 5,* 581-594.

duPre, A. (2000). *Communicating about health: Current issues and perspectives.* Mountain View, CA: Mayfield Publishing.

Gowen, J.W., Schoen C. D., & Sparling, J. (1993). Information needs of parents of young children with special needs. *Journal of Early Intervention, 17*(2), 194-210.

Hadlow, J. & Pitts, M. (1991). The understanding of common health terms by doctors, nurses and patients. *Social Science and Medicine, 32,* 193.

Hall, E. T. (1976). *Beyond culture.* Garden City, NY: Anchor Press/Doubleday.

Hart, A. & Wyatt, S. (2004). The role of the Internet in patient-practitioner relationships: Findings from a qualitative study. *Journal of Medical Internet Research, 6*(3), e36. Retrieved on February 11, 2008, from http://www.jmir.org/2004/3/e36

Jarrett, N. & Payne, S. (1995). A selective review of the literature on nursing-patient communication: Has the patient's contribution been neglected? *Journal of Advanced Nursing, 22,* 72-78.

Johnson, H. C., Renaud, E., Schmidt, D. T., & Stanek, E. J. (1998). Social workers' views of parents of children with mental and emotional disabilities. *Families in Society, 79*(3), 173-187.

Larsen, K. M. & Smith, C. K. (1981). Assessment of nonverbal communication in the patent-physician interview. *Journal of Family Practice, 12,* 481-489.

Ley, P. (1988). *Communicating with patients. Improving communication, satisfaction and compliance.* Chapman and Hall, London.

Lynch, E. W. & Hanson, M. J. (2004). *Developing cross-cultural competence: A guide for working with young children and their families.* Baltimore: Paul H. Brookes Publishing.

McCubbin, H. I. (1983). The family stress process: The double ABCX model of adjustment and adaptation. *Marriage and Family Review, 6*(1), 7-37.

McWilliam, R. A. (1992). *Family-centered intervention planning: A routines-based approach.* Tucson, AZ: Communication Skill Builders.

Mitchell, W. & Sloper, P. (2002). Information that informs rather than alienates families with disabled children: Developing a model of good practice. *Health and Social Care in the Community, 10*(2), 74-81.

Northouse, P. G. & Northouse, L. L. (1985). *Health communication: A handbook for health professionals.* Englewood Cliffs, NJ: Prentice.

O'Hair, H. D., Friedrich, G., & Dixon, L. (2007). *Strategic communication for business and the professions* (5th ed.). Boston: Houghton Mifflin.

Pendleton, D., Schofield, T., Tate, P., & Havelock, P. (1984). *The consultation: An approach to learning and teaching.* Oxford: Oxford University Press.

Robinson, J. D. (1998). Getting down to business: Talk, gaze, and body orientation during openings of doctor-patient consultations. *Human Communication Research, 25,* 97-123.

Romig, D. A. (1996). *Breakthrough teamwork: Outstanding results using structured teamwork.* Chicago: Irwin.

Roter, D. L., Frankel, R. M., Hall, J. A., & Sluyter, D. (2006). The expression of emotion through nonverbal behavior in medical visits. Mechanisms and outcomes. *Journal of General Internal Medicine, 21*(Suppl. 1), S28–S34.

Rupiper, M. & Marvin, C. (2004). Preparing teachers for family-centered services: A survey of preservice curricular content. *Teacher Education and Special Education, 27*(4), 384-395.

Sandall, S., Hemmeter, M. L., Smith, B., & McLean, M. (2005). *DEC Recommended practices: A comprehensive guide.* Missoula, MN: Division of Early Childhood.

Smith, P. M. (2003). *Parenting a child with special needs.* NICHCY News Digest 20, 3rd edition, Washington, DC: National Dissemination System for Children with Disabilities.

Smith, R. C. & Hoppe, R. B. (1991). The patient's story: Integrating the patient- and physician-centered approaches to interviewing. *Annals of Internal Medicine, 115,* 470-477.

Stewart, C. J. & Cash, W. B. (2008). *Interviewing: Principles and practices* (12th ed.). McGraw-Hill.

Street, R. L. & Buller, D. B. (1987). Nonverbal behavior patterns in physician-patient interactions: A functional analysis. *Journal of Nonverbal Behavior, 11,* 234-253.

Suchman, A. L., Markakis, K., Beckman, H. B., & Frankel, R. (1997). A model of empathetic communication in the medical interview. *Journal of the American Medical Association, 277,* 678-683.

Turnbull, A. P., Turbiville, V., & Turnbull, H. R. (2000). Evolution of family-professional partnerships: Collective empowerment as the model for the early twenty-first century. In J. P. Shonkoff & S. J. Meisels (Eds.), *Handbook of early childhood intervention* (2nd ed., pp. 630-650). New York: Cambridge University Press.

Williams, D. (1997). *Communication skills in practice: A practical guide for health professionals.* London: Athenaeum Press.

Winton, P. J. (1988). Effective communication between parents and professionals. In D. B. Bailey & R. J. Simeonsson (Eds.), *Family assessment in early intervention* (pp. 207-228). Columbus, OH: Charles E. Merrill.

Wright, K., Sparks, L., & O'Hair, D. (2008). *Health communication in the 21st century.* Hoboken, NJ: Blackwell Publishing.

Infant and Toddler Portfolios as an Assessment Tool

Considerations When Getting Started

Michaelene M. Ostrosky, Ph.D.

SungYoon Lee, Ph.D.
University of Illinois at Urbana–Champaign

Darcy Ehmen McMahon, M.S.
Potomac Elementary School

Over the past several years, assessment and accountability have become two of the most widely discussed topics in education, including early childhood education and early childhood special education (ECSE) (Arter, Spandel, & Culham, 1995; Division for Early Childhood [DEC], 2007; Grace, Shores, & Brown, 1994; Hyson, 2002; Lankes, 1995; National Association for the Education of Young Children [NAEYC], 2003). As parents become increasingly aware of the importance of development during the early childhood (EC) years, the demand for high-quality, developmentally appropriate programs that meet the needs of their young children has grown (Turnbull, Turnbull, Erwin, & Soodak, 2006). Additionally, those who care for and educate infants, toddlers, and young children with and without disabilities should continue to critically evaluate their programs to ensure that all children gain new skills and knowledge (DEC, NAEYC).

Portfolio development is an assessment process that shows promise for use with infants, toddlers, and preschoolers (Gronlund & Engel, 2001; Jarrett, Browne, & Wallin, 2006; Thompson, Meadan, Fansler, Alber, & Balogh, 2007) as a way to monitor progress and document growth. Many EC and ECSE professionals have tried implementing portfolio assessment in their settings, realizing the benefits as well as challenges. Although some information is available regarding portfolios and how to implement them with infants and toddlers (Jarrett et al.), most information is aimed at using portfolios with children who are preschool age or older (e.g., Batzle, 1992; Campbell, Milbourne, & Silberman, 2001).

The purpose of this article is to share ideas for using portfolios with infants and toddlers. Following a brief discussion of the purposes that infant/toddler portfolios serve, the focus turns to describing four steps that are useful as early interventionists begin creating infant/toddler portfolios. Commonly asked questions are then presented, and differences between portfolios for infants/toddlers and children who are older are highlighted.

What Purposes Do Portfolios Serve?

Several authors have discussed the multiple purposes that portfolios serve (e.g., Brooks, 2003; Danielson & Abrutyn, 1997; Gronlund, 1998; Jarrett et al., 2006). Gronlund and Engel (2001) described how portfolios provide information about infants' and toddlers' growth and development, serve as a resource for teachers and early interventionists to share information with families, and guide interventionists in planning individualized curriculum. Portfolios can be used to monitor progress and outcomes in response to intervention, making them an ideal medium for use in early intervention (EI). Young children feel most comfortable and confident during play and everyday interactions, and portfolios can be used to document children's strengths within natural environments.

Portfolios also provide a format for early interventionists to use as they reflect upon their own strengths and areas of need. For example, looking at artifacts and talking with colleagues about children and their portfolios provides interventionists with opportunities to assess their own practices. Some questions that can help early interventionists evaluate their practice are: What are my goals and what are the infants and toddlers learning in my setting? Do the portfolio artifacts reflect my goals and the children's learning? Am I documenting all areas of learning across all children (e.g., communication, motor, social-emotional, problem-solving skills)? Am I supporting children's individual goals effectively? Are materials and activities that I use and suggest engaging and challenging for infants and toddlers with a range of abilities?

As parents become increasingly aware of the importance of development during the early childhood (EC) years, the demand for high quality, developmentally appropriate programs that meet the needs of their young children has grown.

Portfolios also enable early interventionists, family members, and other team members to review children's progress to date, and assess, as a team, young children's strengths and weaknesses. Team members can gain insight into the context and content of a child's learning as they see artifacts and read anecdotal notes documenting a child's development. For example, family members can see pictures documenting a developmental milestone or emerging skill. Additionally, family members can contribute artifacts that show other team members their child's progress (e.g., videos or pictures of a child cruising around a table at a family picnic). EI providers can review information in a portfolio prior to an individualized family service plan (IFSP) meeting and select concrete examples to use to support their observations. Portfolios also provide a great keepsake for families, documenting an infant's or toddler's growth.

Finally, portfolios may be used to meet licensing criteria for assessment and can be a way to create interest among families about an EI program. Thus, portfolios can meet the needs of a variety of individuals including infants and toddlers, family members, EI providers and other professionals, and program administrators.

What Are the Steps to Creating Portfolios?

Recommended practices highlight the importance of authentic, ongoing assessment methods that are culturally, ethnically, and linguistically responsive (Sandall et al., 2005). Portfolios are one form of assessment that can meet these criteria in EI. The following section provides general information about the portfolio process, including how to start a portfolio, what to collect, and how to organize a portfolio. Before beginning to implement a portfolio system for infants and toddlers, it is important to remember that portfolio development is a process. Thinking about the final product can be overwhelming. The following steps provide a framework for creating a portfolio system for assessment purposes (Gronlund, 1998).

It is important to remember that portfolio development is a process.

Step 1: Organizing an Infant/Toddler Portfolio

Beginning the portfolio process necessitates determining a way to organize the artifacts in a filing or collection system for each infant or toddler. Many EI providers use a filing box or binder to collect and organize artifacts. Filing boxes are useful, because they allow for a variety of sizes of artifacts, but they can take up a lot of space. Binders are easy to keep organized, can be aesthetically pleasing and are portable; however, they also take up much space. Criteria to keep in mind when deciding on a type of portfolio are space, accessibility, confidentiality, and functionality. Selecting a portfolio system also depends on the EI setting, schedule, and an EI provider's preferences.

In addition to dividing artifacts by child, they also need to be organized *within* each child's portfolio binder or file. Some EI providers prefer to arrange the artifacts in chronological order, whereas others choose to organize artifacts by skill type (i.e., drawings over time, photos of caregiver-infant interaction over time). When compiling portfolio artifacts for infants and toddlers, Gronlund and Engel (2001) suggest that interventionists and other team members gather information on the following

six areas of development: (1) shows interest in others; (2) demonstrates self-awareness; (3) accomplishes motor milestones; (4) communicates; (5) acts with purpose and uses tools; and (6) expresses feelings. Information gathered for each area could include photographs, videotapes, anecdotal information, audio recordings, and drawings or paintings. Artifacts should be accompanied by commentary to help with interpretation (Gronlund, 1998). The anecdotal note below might accompany a photograph of 22-month-old Maria, who has developmental delays, reaching toward her EI provider, Juanita.

Maria crawled over to the table and pulled herself up. She looked around the room and saw Juanita sitting with another child 6 feet away. Maria grunted as she looked at Juanita. Juanita said, "Hi, Maria!" Maria reached one arm to Juanita as she held on to the table with her other arm. "Do you want to come to me? Well, come on!" Juanita said. Maria looked at Juanita as she pulled her hand off of the table. She wobbled a bit and then moved her right foot slightly forward. She then took one step with her left foot, wobbled a bit more, and fell onto her bottom. Maria began crying as Juanita clapped and cheered! Juanita walked over to Maria and picked her up. Maria stopped crying. 04/12/2008

Along with anecdotes describing developmental milestones, documentation might include descriptions of favorite materials, activities, family members, and other people. For each artifact, the EI provider might want to document the following to assist with understanding the context of the observation: child-initiated behavior, teacher-initiated activity, novel or familiar task for the infant/toddler, done independently, done with adult guidance or support, amount of effort involved (involved great effort, involved little effort), and time spent. An individual child's strengths or needs may influence the specific areas chosen as a focus for the portfolio.

Three things to remember about organizing an infant/toddler portfolio are: it needs to be systematic (it is obvious where to find and place each artifact); it needs to be functional (how a portfolio is organized should be consistent with how it is used); and it needs to be aesthetically pleasing (presented in a way that families and other team members value). Some EI providers type the information that they include about each artifact for a professional look, whereas others prefer handwritten notes; a systematic format ensures that all artifacts are reader and family friendly.

Step 2: Documenting Within an Infant/Toddler Portfolio

Once the focus and format of the portfolio has been determined, documenting infant/toddler development can begin. The best way to begin documenting it is to find small windows of opportunity throughout the day to write notes about specific incidents witnessed, interactions observed, or materials and activities that engaged the child. Taking pictures helps in remembering things to write about at a later point in time.

Although initially it may be difficult to determine what to write about in a portfolio, with practice, documentation becomes easier. Topics that are pertinent to include in portfolio observations and documentation are the date, who was involved, and details about the context that will help in understanding the artifact. Other things to take in to consideration include adults or children who were nearby or who interacted with the child, important pieces of information that a reader should be aware of (previous contexts, temperament, new skill, or change from a previous artifact). Anecdotal records offer factual, nonjudgmental, descriptive information about an event; they may or may not include "hard evidence," such as artwork, digital photos, and audiotapes. The evaluation of anecdotal records occurs at a later point in the portfolio process. An example of an anecdotal record about a toddler with Down syndrome follows.

Eighteen-month-old Eric was in the block area alone. He had built a tower three blocks high. A 24-month-old peer walked over and laughed as he kicked down Eric's structure. Eric looked at his peer and then began laughing. Eric placed three more blocks on top of each other and waited as he looked at the peer. The peer looked at Eric and then kicked the blocks over once again. Both children laughed. Eric continued to build structures ranging from two to five blocks high; he laughed as his peer kicked over each one. This activity lasted for 8 minutes, and then his peer walked over to the Play-Doh as Eric contin-ued to build independently with blocks. 02/13/2008

Many EI providers express frustration at not having enough time during the day to document children's learning (Kleinert, Kennedy, & Kearns, 1999). This can be especially true in infant and toddler rooms, where EI providers are constantly interacting with young children. There are few opportu-nities to jot down a few words or take a photo without interrupting feeding, diapering, and sleeping routines or children's play. Writing anecdotal notes about infant/toddler learning might best occur during rest time or when rocking sleepy babies. Having paper and a clipboard readily available can make writing anecdotal notes more efficient. Additionally, having one EI provider take pictures as another interacts with the children can help capture important events.

Ensuring that all infants and toddlers have a portfolio full of pertinent information requires planning.

Ensuring that all infants and toddlers have a portfolio full of perti-nent information requires planning. Children's work should be collected with intent and purpose. EI providers might select one or two toddlers each day and see what opportunities for documentation arise. If another child is observed mastering a new skill (i.e., initiating a sign for the first time, sitting up independently, self-feeding), documentation can occur for that child as well. It is, however, important to note that the number of anecdotal records does not mean that a broad range of skills has been assessed. Quality anecdotal notes and artifacts are more important than the quantity of notes and artifacts.

Step 3: Reflecting on Infant/Toddler Portfolios

It is important to periodically review and reflect on the documentation that has been collected. Reflection is one of the most important parts of the portfolio process. Portfolios provide a vehicle through which EI providers can identify and interpret developmen-tal skills that have been mastered or are emerging, skills that a child may start acquiring soon, and ideas for mak-ing the environment conducive to indi-vidual children's needs. By reviewing and interpreting development as it occurs, EI providers can ensure that every infant and toddler makes progress.

Reflection is one of the most important parts of the portfolio process.

To determine what learning is evident in each artifact gathered for a particular infant or toddler, there are a variety of things EI providers should consider when reflecting upon the artifacts. See Box 1 for sample reflective questions. An example of a reflection follows:

Fourteen-month-old Jack clung to Miss Betty after watching his Mom leave the physical therapy room. His ability to cope with separation anxiety and his attachment to his new physical therapist is emerging. 06/24/2008

Box 1
Sample Reflective Questions

What was the infant/toddler working on when engaged in this behavior or activity?

Was the infant/toddler learning a new skill, practicing an emerging skill, or mastering a skill?

Is this activity or behavior typical for infants/toddlers of this age?

What skills should I look for next?

How can I use this information to plan future activities?

According to Gronlund (2001), "The teacher commentary that accompanies the work becomes a critical factor in making a piece informative" (p. 9). Reflection also helps professionals think critically about their own practices as they consider what they select to document, why they select particular artifacts, and how they can best use this information to improve their practice and better help each infant/toddler to meet his/her targeted outcomes. Additionally, reviewing and reflecting upon anecdotal notes and other forms of documentation can assist EI providers in creating opportunities to meet all children's needs.

Step 4: Implementing an Infant/Toddler Portfolio System

At first, implementing a portfolio system with infants and toddlers might appear to be a great deal of work. Over time, however, EI providers learn what things are beneficial and important to document. For example, purposefully taking digital pictures to demonstrate specific skill development is more efficient than haphazardly taking photographs every few weeks with the hope of finding something worthy of placing in a child's portfolio.

As EI providers become skilled at a variety of ways to document infant and toddler learning (e.g., gathering video, audio, or digital recordings, writing notes), strategies for documenting feasibly within the context of busy EI settings emerge (e.g., jotting down notes to help remember an interaction, taking several photos in a row to document the steps of a newly mastered skill, finding consistent times in the day to write about and reflect on children's learning). Even after years of experience using portfolios, few professionals would call themselves experts. Talking with others who have experimented with portfolio assessment is one way to learn from and seek support from those with more experience. Brooks (2003) gathered feedback from professionals with differing levels of portfolio experience. Table 1 provides a summary of commonly asked questions about portfolio development, which was shared by these individuals.

Table 1
Frequently Asked Questions

Frequently asked questions	Answers
What do I write on the anecdotal forms as I observe?	- Record both the ordinary and the extraordinary
	- Record activities that are new and different
	- Report on specific activities and include details
	- Quote children's words/phrases/ conversations
	- Note the time a child spends involved in an activity
	- Set up the scenario you see and follow up with the outcome of the situation
How much should I write on each anecdotal note?	- Write enough to give an account of the activity or action
	- Describe what happened and who was involved, then describe in detail the play or action
	- When using a photograph or art sample, a detailed anecdotal note should accompany it
When noting the developmental skills used, should I list the skills mastered or skills that a child might be gaining experience in during an activity?	- Note skills the child has mastered and those he/she is acquiring
	- Describe listed skills by adding narrative information
How should I report inappropriate behavior?	- Report what happened using professional language
	- Be objective; do not exaggerate

Table 1 (continued)

	- Balance it with reports about activities and behaviors that highlight the child's strengths
What should I record when I see no growth or very limited change in a child over a period of time?	- Continue to collect artifacts that document what the child is doing, even if they seem repetitive
	- Be patient as infants and toddlers' development of some skills may appear to be occurring at a slow rate (i.e., cooperatively interacting with others)
	- Work closely with parents who may document some growth at home or in other natural environments
How do I decide which developmental area an artifact belongs in?	- Ask yourself, "Which developmental area most closely matches the activity and behaviors I have described?"
	- Use professional judgment and/or team decision-making to place each artifact in the area that best matches the observation
Should a consistent EI provider be responsible for the same children's portfolios for the duration of the time the child is in EC settings?	- This is a program-level decision
	- Consider the benefits of having more than one perspective
	- Work flexibly given the program's staffing and philosophy
How can I keep track of the materials I have collected and determine what I still need?	- This is a personal choice
	- Place a file box in a spot easily accessible to all staff but out of the children's reach. Then each day as artifacts are collected, they can be placed in the children's files
	- Keep a running list all of the items collected for each developmental area in a file, updating it by adding new items collected at the end of each week
	- Collect data for a month, checking the children's files to assess developmental areas in which they still need artifacts
	- Gather all of the blank anecdotal forms you will need at the beginning of each month and label them with the children's names. At the end of each day, transfer any forms containing observations, along with artifacts, into the children's files

Table 1 (continued)

Is there a way to make portfolios less time consuming?	- A good organizational structure is of utmost importance
	- Knowing what has been collected and what types of activities need to be observed will help with the task of observing and gathering artifacts
	- Occasionally set up activities that are sure to provide artifacts for the portfolios
	- Organizational skills and observation/anecdote writing skills will improve with experience, saving time and energy
How many artifacts should each portfolio include?	- There is no magic number
Do portfolio entries need to be typed?	- Typing is not necessary, but neatness and correct grammar, punctuation, and sentence structures are needed
How do I establish effective family/professional partnerships?	- Provide opportunities for parents to contribute to the portfolio and/or make recommendations on how information is organized, displayed, etc.
	- Show parents and other team members how the portfolio is organized, describe the areas of development, then share it with them as you draw their attention to specific artifacts of importance
	- Show them the developmental summaries
	- Take time to discuss areas of significant progress and suggestions for supporting continued growth
	- Allow time for questions and listen to anecdotes from home
How can the portfolio be used in team meetings and program planning?	- Team members can bring it to meetings, highlighting specific artifacts to support discussions of child strengths or areas of concern

Note. EI = early intervention; EC = early childhood. Adapted from Brooks, J. D. (with Trouth, D.). (2003). *Developmental portfolios: A guide to informal, observational assessment of children's developmental progress.* Unpublished manuscript. University of Illinois at Urbana–Champaign.

Are There Differences Between Infant/Toddler Portfolios and Portfolios for Older Children?

When considering whether differences exist between infant and toddler portfolios and portfolios for older children, the answer is both yes and no. In general, completed portfolios look similar and include similar things.

However, because developmental differences exist among infants, toddlers, and preschoolers, the information included in the portfolios varies. Differences include documentation about how and what children learn, along with how children communicate their knowledge. These differences impact how professionals collect information for portfolios.

Differences in How Children Learn

From birth, children gather information from the world around them through exploration and interactions. Using their senses, skills, and experiences, they accumulate new information. For young children with special needs, this exploration and interactive style may take on a different form as new information and skills emerge (i.e., toddlers who are blind tend to bring new objects to their mouths as a way to explore them).

As they develop, infants and toddlers need concrete experiences, whereas preschoolers are beginning to think abstractly and call upon past experiences to make meaning of new knowledge. In terms of portfolio documentation for infants and toddlers, this means that EI providers will document learning by interpreting interactions between infants or toddlers and people or materials in the environment.

Differences in What Children Are Learning

It is imperative that professionals have a strong background in typical and atypical development when creating infant and toddler portfolios. For example, an EI provider must recognize when an infant or toddler fails to achieve developmental milestones around communication development, despite having no physical disability or cognitive delay. It is impossible to monitor progress or assess skills and knowledge if one does not have a strong understanding of what typical development looks like. In a similar vein, professionals must understand characteristics of disabilities and realize that movement, communication, self-care, and cognition may be affected in different ways by the same disability and in different (or sometimes similar) ways across disability conditions. For example, the motor development of all toddlers with cerebral palsy does not look the same and therefore requires different accommodations, instruction, or treatment (and subsequently different types of portfolio entries) from EI providers. One child might have an emphasis on self-care such as feeding, due to motor issues around her arms and hands, whereas another child might have an emphasis on skills such as running outdoors, due to possible impact on his leg muscles and large motor development.

When focusing on the infant and toddler period, one quickly realizes that children typically achieve many major developmental milestones during the first 3 years of life, including walking, talking, and beginning peer interactions, to name a few. Infants begin to develop some initial skills; preschoolers work on mastering skills and building upon previously learned skills. For example, whereas infants learn to make and repeat sounds, preschoolers work on building vocabulary and learning the meaning of words. Whereas toddlers begin to learn about sharing and playing with others, preschoolers begin using different strategies to maintain interactions with friends and to handle anger and conflict.

Behaviors often reveal what a child knows or does not know; the observant EI provider notices these behaviors and skillfully interprets them. For example, a toddler who does not know how to tell another child that she

is in his space may bite, or an infant who realizes that he can control his hands might reach out and touch a mobile. Additionally, an infant who crawls away from her teacher might demonstrate large muscle control along with emotional competence through perceptions of feeling safe and secure enough in the environment to move away from the adult.

Differences in How Children Communicate Knowledge and Skills

Infants and toddlers spend a great deal of time exploring the world around them. Using their senses, they learn how things work and what it means to live in this world. As they gain knowledge and skills, infants and toddlers are willing to try new things. For example, an 8-month-old might pick up a cloth book, shake it, gaze at it, move it around with her other hand, hold it close to her face, and put it in her mouth. Although the adult may not know exactly what the child is thinking, it is clear that she is demonstrating a variety of skills.

As infants begin to learn that communication has meaning and that they can influence their environments by communicating, an observant EI provider will notice the purposeful and deliberate ways infants and toddlers use communication. There are a variety of ways that infants and toddlers communicate, including verbal forms (e.g., babbling, sounds, words) and nonverbal forms (e.g., facial expressions, gestures, pointing, clapping, sign language, reaching, hitting). It is important to observe carefully how infants and toddlers with and without disabilities interact with the world in order to document what and how they are learning.

Conclusion

One of the most critical pieces that must be in place when implementing an infant/toddler portfolio system is a strong focus on relationships. Relationships support young children as they work on attachment, autonomy, and self-awareness, and this focus on relationships can help EI providers understand each child as an individual. Without knowledge about each individual child, professionals cannot possibly know what skills are new, emerging, or mastered. The portfolio "is intended to create a portrait of the child as a learner—and to tell a story about the child's learning over time" (Meisels, Dichtelmiller, Jablon, Dorfman, & Marsden, 1997).

Although a variety of resources that provide an abundance of information on different aspects of portfolios is available, for professionals who work with infants and toddlers, information is limited. When getting started, Gronlund (1998) suggests that administrators and EI providers "need to recognize their own learning process. Portfolio assessment involves many decisions. Learning what makes the most informative piece or which learning objectives are most easily documented takes time and practice" (p. 10). The benefits of portfolios as an assessment tool for infants and toddlers are numerous. As Jarrett and her colleagues (2006) stated, infant and toddler portfolios meet recommended practices for assessment and can address the eight critical indicators of quality early childhood assessment espoused by Neisworth and Bagnato (2005). Portfolios are an excellent way for EI providers and other professionals to document that all infants and toddlers in their care are learning and developing.

Note
You may contact Micki Ostrosky by e-mail at ostrosky@illinois.edu

References

Arter, J. A., Spandel, V., & Culham, R. (1995). *Portfolios for assessment and instruction.* Greensboro, NC: ERIC Document Reproduction Services, ED388890.

Batzle, J. (1992). *Portfolio assessment and evaluation: Developing and using portfolios in the K-6 classroom.* Cypress, CA: Creative Teaching Press.

Brooks, J. D. (with Trouth, D.). (2003). *Developmental portfolios: A guide to informal, observational assessment of children's developmental progress.* Unpublished manuscript. University of Illinois at Urbana-Champaign.

Campbell, P. H., Milbourne, S. A., & Silverman, C. (2001). Strengths-based child portfolios: A professional development activity to alter perspectives of children with special needs. *Topics in Early Childhood Special Education, 21*(3), 152-161.

Danielson, C. & Abrutyn, L. (1997). *An introduction to using portfolios in the classroom.* Alexandria, VA: Association for Supervision and Curriculum Development.

Division for Early Childhood. (2007). *Promoting positive outcomes for children with disabilities: Recommendations for curriculum, assessment and program evaluation.* Retrieved June 15, 2008, from http://www.decsped.org./pdf/positionpapers/Prmtg_Pos_Outcomes_Companion_Paper.pdf

Grace, C., Shores, E. F., & Brown, M. H. (1994). *The portfolio and its use as a developmentally appropriate assessment of young children.* Little Rock, AR: Southern Early Childhood Association.

Gronlund, G. (1998). Portfolios as an assessment tool: Is collection of work enough? *Young Children, 53*(3), 4-10.

Gronlund, G. & Engel, B. (2001). *Focused portfolios a complete assessment for the young child.* St. Paul, MN: Redleaf Press.

Hyson, M. (2002). "Huh?" "Eek!" "Help": Three perspectives on early childhood assessment. *Young Children, 57*(1), 62-64.

Jarrett, M. H., Browne, B. C., & Wallin C. M. (2006). Using portfolio assessment to document developmental progress of infants and toddlers. *Young Exceptional Children, 10*(1), 22-32.

Kleinert, H. L., Kennedy, S., & Kearns, J. F. (1999). The impact of alternate assessments: A statewide teacher survey. *Journal of Special Education, 33,* 93-102.

Lankes, A. M. D. (1995). *Electronic portfolios a new idea in assessment.* Syracuse, NY: ERIC Clearinghouse on Information & Technology, ED390377.

Meisels, S., Dichtelmiller, M., Jablon, J., Dorfman, A., & Marsden, D. (1997). *Work sampling in the classroom: A teacher's manual. The Work Sampling System.* Ann Arbor, NI: Rebus.

National Association for the Education of Young Children (NAEYC). (1998). *Accreditation criteria & procedures of the National Association for the Education of Young Children—1998 edition.* Washington, DC: Author.

National Association for the Education of Young Children (NAEYC). (2003). *Early childhood curriculum, assessment, and program evaluation: A joint position statement of the National Association for the Education of Young Children and the National Association of Early Childhood Specialists in State Departments of Education.* Retrieved June 15, 2008, from http://www.naeyc.org/about/positions/pdf/StandlCurrAss.pdf

Thompson, J. R., Meadan, H., Fansler, K. W., Alber, S. B., & Balogh, P. A. (2007). Family assessment portfolios: A new way to jumpstart family/school collaboration. *Teaching Exceptional Children, 39*(6), 19-25.

Turnbull, A., Turnbull, R., Erwin, E. J., & Soodak, L. C. (2006). *Families, professionals, and exceptionality* (5th ed.). Upper Saddle River, NJ: Merrill Prentice Hall.

Conducting Home Visits With an Explicit Theory of Change

Kere Hughes, Ph.D.,

Carla A. Peterson, Ph.D.,
Iowa State University

Sarah, a home visitor, walks into Janet's office, tears streaming down her face. Janet, her supervisor, wondering what could be wrong, sits down and asks Sarah to tell her. After gaining some composure, Sarah explains she had completed her last home visit prior to Jason's transition to the local Part B preschool program. As Sarah was leaving, Jason's mother, Linda, stopped her to ask one final question, "Can you tell me how to teach him new things? I want him to be ready for school." "I didn't know what to say," wailed Sarah. "Isn't that what I've been doing twice a month for 2 years? I have been modeling teaching strategies for Linda!" Both Sarah and Janet are stumped. "You clearly had great rapport with Linda, and Jason loved you," consoled Janet. "That's what I thought too," Sarah said, as she recalled how during home visits she had spent time talking with Linda about Jason's development and using evidence-based instructional strategies to interact with Jason. "I even went out of my way to get to know the people and places in Jason's life," Sarah despaired, "What did I do wrong?"

This scenario is all too frequent when we, as home visitors, don't have a clear focus for what we are doing, how we are doing it, and most important, why we are doing what we do. Rather than a particular model of intervention, home visiting is a method of service delivery. Home visiting programs have a long history, provide families with many types of support for many different reasons, and are used widely (Gomby, Culross, & Behrman, 1999). Part C programs provide early intervention services for families of children with special needs; more than 80% of Part C early intervention services are provided via home visiting (Bailey, Scarborough, & Hebbeler, 2003). Parents as Teachers programs focus on early parent-child interactions and school readiness (Wagner & Clayton, 1999; Wagner, Spiker, & Linn, 2002), Early Head Start programs target a wide range of goals for families with young children who are living in poverty (Raikes et al., 2006), and some programs (e.g., Healthy Families

America) target very specific goals such as prevention of child maltreatment (Daro & Harding, 1999). However, a program's goals do not necessarily dictate specific strategies to achieve those goals, overall or with individual families.

What We Know About Home Visiting Programs

Findings from evaluations of home visiting programs over the past 20 years provide some evidence for the effectiveness of home visiting programs. In general, families participating in home visiting programs tend to fare better than similar families who do not receive those services (Sweet & Appelbaum, 2004). Overall effects of home visiting programs, however, are mixed, modest in size and scope (Gomby et al., 1999), and sometimes limited to specific groups (e.g., teen mothers). Unfortunately, little evidence is available to help us understand how home visiting services are individualized to meet families' needs or the relationships among specific aspects of home visiting services and intervention outcomes (Peterson, Luze, Eshbaugh, Jeon, & Kantz, 2007).

We do know that some home visiting programs have helped parents increase knowledge and skills and improve attitudes related to parenting, as well as enhance their own well-being in a number of ways (e.g., reduce maternal depression, reduce and/or delay subsequent births, increase education) (Brooks-Gunn, Berlin, & Fuligni, 2000; Olds, Kitzman, Cole, & Robinson, 1997). Also, some home visiting programs have been associated with a variety of positive child outcomes (Butz et al., 2001; Heinicke et al., 2001; Olds et al., 2002). Implementation integrity, as well as time focused on child development rather than family-related issues or relationship development, was associated with more positive child outcomes among families receiving home-based services in the Early Head Start Research and Evaluation Project (Love et al., 2005; Raikes et al., 2006). Especially vulnerable mothers (e.g., teen mothers, mothers with little education) were more likely to be highly engaged when the home visitor interacted with both her and her child simultaneously; unfortunately, this happened during only a small portion of most home visits (Peterson et al., 2007). Families participating in home visiting programs receive, on average, only half of intended vis-

A well-articulated theory of change specifies a program's goals, as well as the specific avenues through which a program is expected to work.

its, and many families (20% to 67% in recent evaluations) drop out of home-based programs before they receive the full amount of intended intervention (Gomby et al., 1999). Families who drop out early tend to accrue fewer

A theory of change can be a very useful tool to guide a variety of program activities.

benefits from participation (Roggman, Cook, Peterson, & Staerkel, 2008). Researchers and interventionists alike often point to a lack of engagement and early drop out being due to a lack of program "fit" or meaningfulness (either actual or perceived) for many families (Gomby, 2007).

Theory of Change

A well-articulated theory of change specifies a program's goals, as well as the specific avenues through which a program is expected to work (Weiss, 1995). In other words, a theory of change describes how participation in specific program activities will lead to attainment of specified goals and how program staff will interact with participants to target identified goals, thus improving program fit. Today, most home visiting programs have embraced a family-centered, culturally responsive philosophy; early interventionists strive to work collaboratively with family members, providing them the support they need to nurture their children's development. The theory of change underlying this approach is that loving, responsive parent-child interactions that occur within the context of daily routines provide optimal learning opportunities, and early interventionists promote children's development indirectly through their efforts to facilitate parent-child interactions. Coaching strategies are an important tool interventionists use to support parents' interactions with their children while simultaneously facilitating their use of specific learning strategies related to their individualized goals (Hanft, Rush, & Shelden, 2003). A theory of change can be a very useful tool to guide a variety of program activities, including staff recruitment, training, and support; interactions with families; internal or external evaluations; and reports to funding agencies. Unfortunately, many home visiting programs operate without a clear theory of change, and program stakeholders often have different visions and fail to work in concert with each other. For example, a board member may believe that home visitors are helping parents overcome stress, the program coordinator may be focused on child development outcomes, and the home visitor is working with the parent to enhance the safety of her home. Any of these might be appropriate goals and activities, but it is helpful if programs monitor the match among their program goals,

intervention activities, and training and technical assistance provided to staff members. Additionally, program staff members must collaborate with family participants to monitor the match between family goals and program activities. Without these efforts, programs can become less-comprehensive versions of their original design, program effects can be weakened, and families may leave the program early (Gomby, 2007).

Let's take a closer look at Sarah's work with Linda and Jason in light of this information. Sarah is an early childhood special educator who conducts home visits with families of infants and toddlers with special needs. For the past few years, Sarah has been learning about the importance of children's participation in natural environments and trying to provide learning opportunities for children within the context of their daily routines (Dunst et al., 2001). Sarah and Linda worked together with other team members to establish the goals on Jason's individualized family service plan (IFSP); for example, one goal is to gain muscle strength and balance in order to increase movement and eventual walking. Also, Sarah and Linda identified routines where intervention strategies could be used to address this goal. Specifically, they decided that providing more space and opportunities for movement when the family tends to relax in the living room could be helpful during the evenings. They also discussed how specific play opportunities, such as playing on the swings or supporting Jason as he "walks" across the swinging bridge at the park across the street, could be used for assisting him develop strength and balance skills.

Sarah's twice-monthly visits with Jason and Linda were typically an hour long. Sarah started each visit by entering the home respectfully and discussing the week in order to learn Linda's perceptions about Jason's development or any special concerns Linda had about their current circumstances. Sarah asked specifically what Jason had been doing and how he had been feeling. After this initial conversation, Sarah interacted with Jason in positive, child-directed activities to model appropriate teaching strategies for Linda. Sarah also engaged Jason in some caregiving routines like eating and dressing. Linda watched closely as Sarah interacted with Jason and occasionally talked about family-related issues. During each visit, Sarah focused on providing learning opportunities pertinent to the movement goal outlined in the family's IFSP. At the end of each visit, Sarah asked Linda if she had any questions and scheduled their next visit.

Many positive things happened during these home visits, and Sarah felt confident that Linda was capable of providing learning opportunities to Jason in between visits. Unfortunately, several critical elements related to effective home visiting were not present. An underlying problem in this situation may well rest in an underarticulated theory of change to guide Sarah and Linda through the process of early intervention.

Transfer of Intervention

Central to recommended practice for early intervention is recognition that the parent(s) and caregiver(s), rather than the early interventionist, are the primary agents of change. As described above, the theory of change guiding this approach to providing services in natural environments is that the interventionist plays an indirect role by supporting the parents through providing information, facilitating access to resources, identifying appropriate learning opportunities, and facilitating the parents' effective interactions with their child both during and between intervention visits. This approach is based on a large and growing body of research that has identified the many contexts, or places, where learning occurs and the dramatic number of opportunities for children to gain and practice skills throughout the typical day (Dunst, Hamby, Trivette, Raab, & Bruder, 2000; Dunst et al., 2001). This "transfer of intervention" to parents is a relatively new concept for many interventionists and may be a shift in the way they do business.

The interventionist plays an indirect role by supporting the parents.

Additionally, many interventionists will meet families where the parents' interactions with their children are not always sensitive and responsive. Interventionists may need support from mental health professionals to gain knowledge and skills related to adult learning strategies to meet the challenges they face when working with these families.

In further discussion, Sarah and Janet identify that their program is truly tied to family-centered, naturalistic practices. "I am determined that the families I work with will be able to provide the learning opportunities that we identify together as being important to their children," says Sarah. "But I'm not exactly sure what to say or do differently. I focus on everyday routines and using the family's own toys and household objects, and I also work hard to be sure that the strategies I include are ones that are tied to the goals and outcomes on the IFSP. I don't understand why this doesn't seem to be working. Parents just don't seem to want to understand." Janet is also determined, so they work together to find some specific strategies that will help Sarah be more explicit with families about the program's theory of change and how her services might help support the parents to provide learning opportunities for their children throughout the day. As Sarah and Janet examine the literature on recommended practices with infants and toddlers, they find several helpful articles about providing naturalistic, routines-based services.

These articles discuss a variety of ways to help identify appropriate routines, to provide meaningful experiences for children (Woods, Kashinath, & Goldstein, 2004), and to write IFSP outcomes focused on daily routines (Jung, 2007). This information is not new to Sarah. Many of these practices are things she already does with families. However, within this literature, they identified some key components to making an intended transfer of intervention explicit to parents. These components focused primarily on engaging parents actively in activities during the home visits and using adult learning strategies. Sarah realized this was what was missing in her practice. Like many early interventionists, Sarah had never received training on adult learning strategies and felt a little uncomfortable "teaching" parents. Specific strategies that can be used to work collaboratively with parents are critical to the explicit transfer of intervention.

Helping parents realize the various learning opportunities available to their children each day and the importance of their roles in supporting their children's development is the essence of the transfer of intervention. The point is not to have parents become interventionists; parents' most important role will always be parenting their children. When successfully carried out, however, the transfer of intervention provides parents with the knowledge and skills needed to capitalize on the multitude of opportunities inherent in the daily routines of children and families. Not all parents view themselves as their child's teacher; however, parents receiving services desire to enhance their child's development. Daily caregiving routines provide a natural and meaningful context for parents to facilitate the development of their infants and toddlers. In this light, the transfer of intervention is conceptually and practically meaningful to families from a diversity of backgrounds. Several strategies, used together, can help parents understand the intended transfer of intervention and build effective partnerships between parents and interventionists. Included among these strategies are (1) describing the program's theory of change at the onset of intervention, (2) giving and receiving information about intervention activities occurring between visits, and (3) triadic interaction (McCallum & Yates, 1994; i.e., engaging parents in interactions with their child during home visits with multiple opportunities to practice skills, learn about the purposes of their actions, and receive coaching). Triadic interaction strategies are central to facilitating the transfer of intervention desired.

Daily caregiving routines provide a natural and meaningful context for parents to facilitate the development of their infants and toddlers.

Describing the Theory of Change

It is critical that the expectations of both the interventionist and the parents are clearly articulated at the beginning of the intervention relationship. Providing a visual depiction of how intervention is expected to work, along with an open and honest discussion about the roles of each person, can influence intervention efforts positively. Figure 1 might be used to explain to parents this model of early intervention. The triadic interactions are highlighted to explain the roles that the provider and parent play and how activities during home visits can be used to advance the parent's competence and confidence, as well as the child's developmental abilities. When families have a history of receiving services from providers who direct all the activities in the visit and interact directly with the child themselves, the parent may have a difficult time adjusting to a naturalistic and parent-focused intervention without such explanation. In addition, parents who do not have a clear understanding of their role in intervention may view home visits as an opportunity to complete other tasks while their child is occupied with the service provider.

Figure 1
Triadic Interaction

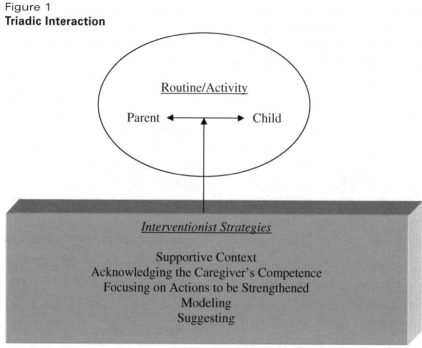

Adapted from McCollum, J. A. & Yates, T. (1994). Dyad as focus, triad as means: A family-centered approach to supporting parent-child interactions. *Infants and Young Children, 6*(4), 54-63.

Information Exchange

In order to determine if the transfer of intervention is actually happening, information must be shared between the parent and interventionist about strategies being used between visits and the child's response to those strategies (Therapists as Collaborative Team Members for Infant/ Toddler Community Services, 2008). A clear and precise agenda could be given to the parent about when, where, how, and—very important— why particular strategies could be used during the time between visits. A simple, straightforward method for the parent to collect information about the frequency and quality of strategies used could be established to facilitate these discussions. For example, one could use a simple notepad prompting the parent to tally each time a strategy was used and a "+" or "−" to circle indicating how well the parent felt the strategy worked. In some instances, it might be easiest for a parent to do this on a prominently displayed calendar. It is important for the parent to be involved in determining how information will be gathered. Some parents will be very interested in writing about the experience; others may only want to gather very basic information. Some parents may not be able to record information systematically, and the early interventionist may need to engage the parent in a conversation to acquire anecdotal notes regarding use of strategies.

Triadic Interactions

Triadic interaction occurs when the parent, child, and early interventionist are all actively participating around the common goal of facilitating dyadic interactions between the parent and child. McCollum and Yates (1994) identify several key elements to building successful triadic interactions including a supportive context that promotes playful interaction, acknowledging the caregiver's competence, focusing on competencies or actions to be strengthened, modeling actions to be learned, and suggesting specific strategies the parent should use with the child. The early interventionist can explain these elements to the parent. In triadic interaction the early interventionist takes the roles of collaborative consultant, coach, and observer rather than teaching directly. The strategies listed above are on a continuum from low (supporting playful interaction) to high (suggesting specific strategies) levels of directiveness by the interventionist. The level of directiveness the interventionist uses is tied to the skills and confidence of the parent with whom he or she is working. Providing a relaxed environment and selecting routines identified by parents can enhance the meaningfulness of the activity for the parent and set the stage for effective interactions. Avoiding direct physical contact with the child and instead watching and talking the parent through the routines and strategies, emphasizing parent strengths, and then making suggestions for the interaction is an effective way of communicating the importance of the parent's role during the intervention process.

Direct physical modeling should be used sparingly, with discretion, and with the parent's consent or at the parent's suggestion. This way, there is explicit communication about what the interventionist is trying to show the parent. In addition, after direct modeling, having the parent demonstrate the strategy with appropriate coaching support is important. This will help ensure the parent understands how to implement the specific strategy and feels confident using it in daily routines.

A New Family—A Fresh Start

Sarah feels ready to make some changes to her practice, considering carefully how she can describe the theory of change guiding early intervention, exchange information with the parent, and use triadic interaction strategies. Sarah and the intervention team write the IFSP document, which outlines the goals that are important to Terry and her baby, Emmy, and discuss strategies that they would like to see implemented. Sarah is the primary interventionist for this family and will conduct the majority of home visits. During an initial home visit, Sarah meets with Terry and Emmy and explains how early intervention services are designed to support parents in their efforts to provide learning opportunities that will help their children grow and develop and will also help their family routines go more smoothly. Sarah conducts a routines-based interview (McWilliam & Clingenpeel, 2003) with Terry to identify daily routines that can use some support and also routines and activities that are particularly enjoyable for Terry and Emmy. The routines-based interview leads the parent through a series of questions about routines and activities from waking up in the morning until bedtime. The interviewer asks questions about how engaged and independent the child is during the routine, the child's social relationships, and how satisfied the parent is with the routine. The interview also helps identify whether the routine is particularly difficult. The interview provides interventionists with extensive information to guide the selection of routines and strategies to use with the family. Let's take a look at a home visit with Sarah, Terry, and Emmy where the elements of triadic interaction are made explicit to the parent.

Sarah enters the home and greets Terry and Emmy as they are having lunch. Prior to the visit, Sarah and Terry identified lunch as a daily routine that is somewhat difficult because Emmy spends a lot of the time crying during meals. One of the objectives on Emmy's IFSP is to communicate her wants and needs by using words or gestures rather than crying or screaming.

Sarah positions herself so that she can see the interaction between Terry and Emmy and observes for a little while. She notices that Emmy cries when she wants something and Terry appears to be frustrated. Terry comments, "I just don't know what she wants." Sarah and Terry talk briefly about how children communicate at this age, that communication begins with gestures, and that they may want to try some techniques to help Emmy to begin communicating in positive ways. Sarah also points out that Terry seems to be able to read Emmy's nonverbal cues and that she understands why this must be frustrating. Sarah teaches Terry the sign for more *and also shows Emmy with some hand-over-hand assistance. Terry identifies some key foods that Emmy really likes and they discuss how to use that for opportunities to sign for* more. *Sarah shows Terry how to pair the sign with the word* more *and how to use appropriate wait time to get Emmy to respond prior to giving her more. Sarah then asks Terry to show her this strategy, which she does, to everyone's delight.*

Once the lunch routine is over, Sarah and Terry discuss how this same strategy can be used during other daily routines and activities. Terry says that Emmy loves it when she blows on her belly, and Sarah asks to see this activity. Sarah points out how much Emmy is enjoying this activity with Terry. Sarah then explains how to use wait time and signing during this activity to get Emmy to use the sign she has just learned and eventually transition to words. Terry tries this strategy, and Emmy signs more *when she wants another belly blow. Sarah suggests that Terry try this strategy during meals and play time and write some simple notes about how it went between visits. Sarah also discusses some other issues related to bookkeeping and scheduling. Then, they jointly decide to follow up at the next visit with more sign language and that Sarah will bring information about more signs Terry can help Emmy learn to use.*

As Sarah drives back to her office, she reflects on the home visit with Terry and Emmy. After watching Terry, Sarah is confident that she will follow through with signing between visits. Sarah anticipates that Terry will find other opportunities to use the same strategy throughout the day. Terry not only understands how to use signs and appropriate wait time with Emmy, she understands why, when, and where she can use these strategies.

Many programs and interventionists are transitioning away from a teacher-directed approach to service delivery. Clearly articulating a theory of change for and with all stakeholders (e.g., parents, interventionists, administrators) will be critical to facilitate implementation of a naturalistic, routines-based, culturally sensitive approach to supporting families through home visiting. This approach will assist program staff members exchange information about the intervention process and engage in triadic interactions designed to help parents support their children's optimal development and their own enjoyment of parent-child interactions.

Note

Corresponding author: You may contact Kere Hughes by e-mail at kereh@iastate.edu

References

Bailey, D., Scarborough, A., & Hebbeler, K. (2003). *Families' first experiences with early intervention: National early intervention longitudinal study.* (Report No. NEILS-R-2). (ERIC Document Reproduction Service No. ED476293). SRI International, Menlo Park, CA.

Brooks-Gunn, J., Berlin, L. J., & Fuligni, A. S. (2000). Early childhood intervention programs: What about the family? In J. P. Shonkoff & S. J. Meisels (Eds.), *Handbook on early childhood intervention* (2nd ed., pp. 549-588). New York: Cambridge University Press.

Butz, A. M., Pulsifer, M., Marano, N., Belcher, H., Lears, M. K., & Royal, R. (2001). Effectiveness of a home intervention for perceived child behavioral problems and parenting stress in children with in utero drug exposure. *Archives of Pediatrics and Adolescent Medicine, 155,* 1029-1037.

Daro, D. & Harding, K. (1999). Healthy Families America: Using research to enhance practice. *The Future of Children, 9,* 152-176.

Dunst, C. J., Bruder, M. B., Trivette, C. M., Hamby, D., Raab, M., & McLean, M. (2001). Characteristics and consequences of everyday natural learning opportunities. *Topics in Early Childhood Special Education, 21,* 68-92.

Dunst, C. J., Hamby, D., Trivette, C. M., Raab, M., & Bruder, M. B. (2000). Everyday family and community life and children's naturally occurring learning opportunities. *Journal of Early Intervention, 23,* 151-164.

Gomby, D. S. (2007). The promise and limitations of home visiting: Implementing effective programs. *Child Abuse & Neglect, 31,* 793-799.

Gomby, D. S., Culross, P. L., & Behrman, R. E. (1999). Home visiting: Recent program evaluations—Analysis and recommendations. *The Future of Children, 9,* 4-26.

Hanft, B., Rush, D., & Shelden, M. (2003). *Coaching families and colleagues in early childhood.* Baltimore: Brookes.

Heinicke, C. M., Goorsky, M., Moscov, S., Dudley, K., Gordon, J., Schneider, C., et al. (2000). Relationship-based intervention with at-risk mothers: Factors affecting variations in outcome. *Infant Mental Health Journal, 21,* 133-155.

Jung, L. A. (2007). Writing individualized family service plan strategies that fit into the routine. *Young Exceptional Children, 10,* 2-9.

Love, J. M., Kisker, E. E., Ross, C., Raikes, H., Constantine, J., Boller, K., et al. (2005). The effectiveness of Early Head Start for 3-year-old children and their parents: Lessons for policy and programs. *Developmental Psychology, 41,* 885-901.

McCollum, J. A. & Yates, T. (1994). Dyad as focus, triad as means: A family-centered approach to supporting parent-child interactions. *Infants and Young Children, 6*(4), 54-63.

McWilliam, R. & Clingenpeel, B. (2003). *Functional intervention planning: The routines-based interview.* Retrieved April 8, 2008, from http://www.collaboratingpartners.com/docs/R_Mcwilliam/RBI%20Flyer%20April%202005.pdf

Olds, D. L., Kitzman, H., Cole, R., & Robinson, J. (1997). Theoretical foundations of a program of home visitation for pregnant women and parents of young children. *Journal of Community Psychology, 25,* 9-25.

Olds, D. L., Robinson, J., O'Brien, R., Luckey, D. W., Pettitt, L. M., Henderson, C. R., et al. (2002). Home visiting by nurses and by paraprofessionals: A randomized controlled trial. *Pediatrics, 110,* 486-496.

Peterson, C. A., Luze, G. J., Eshbaugh, E. M., Jeon, H., & Kantz, K. R. (2007). Enhancing parent-child interactions through home visiting: Promising practice or unfulfilled promise? *Journal of Early Intervention, 29,* 119-140.

Raikes, H., Green, B., Atwater, J., Kisker, E., Constantine, J., & Chazan-Cohen, R. (2006). Involvement in Early Head Start home visiting services: Demographic predictors and relations to child and parent outcomes. *Early Childhood Research Quarterly, 21,* 2-24.

Roggman, L., Cook, G., Peterson, C. A., Raikes, H. A., Staerkel, E. (2008). Who drops out of Early Head Start home-based programs. *Early Education and Development, 19,* 574-599.

Sweet, M. & Appelbaum, M. (2004). Is home visiting an effective strategy? A meta-analytic review of home visiting programs for families with young children. *Child Development, 75,* 1435-1456.

Therapists as Collaborative Team Members for Infant/Toddler Community Services. (2008). Retrieved July 15, 2008, from http://tactics.fsu.edu/family.html

Wagner, M. & Clayton, S. (1999). The Parents as Teachers program: Results from two demonstrations. *The Future of Children, 9,* 91-115.

Wagner, M., Spiker, D., & Linn, M. I. (2002). The effectiveness of the Parents as Teachers program with low-income parents and children. *Topics in Early Childhood Special Education, 22,* 67-81.

Weiss, C. H. (1995). Nothing as practical as good theory: Exploring theory-based evaluation for comprehensive community initiatives for children and families. In J. P. Connell (Ed.), *New approaches to evaluating community initiatives: Concepts, methods, contexts* (pp. 65-92). Queenstown, MD: Aspen Institute.

Woods, J., Kashinath, S., & Goldstein, H. (2004). Effects of embedding caregiver-implemented teaching strategies in daily routines on children's communication outcomes. *Journal of Early Intervention, 26,* 175-193.

Home-Visit Early Intervention Practices with Families and Their Infants Who Have Multiple Disabilities

Deborah Chen, Ph.D.,
California State University, Northridge

M. Diane Klein, Ph.D., C.C.C.-S.L.P.,
California State University, Los Angeles

Infants identified as having multiple disabilities are an extremely diverse and heterogeneous population. These infants often have complex needs, unclear diagnoses, and low-incidence disabilities that require the services of multiple disciplines. Providing high-quality, coordinated early intervention services to these infants and their families within the natural environment of the home can be very challenging. Service providers may be employed by different agencies, vary in levels of experience and expertise with infants who have multiple disabilities, and use diverse, even conflicting, intervention approaches with these children and families. In this article, we discuss considerations for providing home-visiting services to the family and their infant with multiple disabilities and offer some guidance for the delivery of services in a manner that will meet the family's priorities and concerns, maximize resources, fit within family routines, and promote interactions with the infant.

Factors That Shape Early Intervention Services

Home visiting in early intervention with families of infants who have significant disabilities is a complicated process that is influenced by many factors. Figure 1 provides a conceptual model (Klein, in press) that illustrates the dynamic interactions among the key variables of home visiting, including the characteristics of the child and family, the purpose and philosophy of the home visiting program, the training and experience of service providers, and the strategies and activities used in home visits.

Figure 1
A Conceptual Framework of Early Intervention Home Visiting

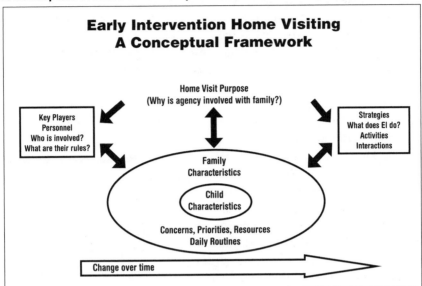

Early intervention services are influenced by the requirements of Part C of the Individuals with Disabilities Education Act, which include an individualized family service plan (IFSP) that identifies the family's concerns, priorities, and resources related to their infant's development; the natural environments in which early intervention services will be provided; and a service coordinator who will be responsible for the implementation of the plan and coordination of services (Bruder & Dunst, 2008; Jung, 2007; Raab, 2004). The overall goal and guiding philosophy of early intervention with infants with disabilities (Sandall, Hemmeter, Smith, & McLean, 2005) is to facilitate the infant's development by supporting caregivers through providing information and training within daily routines and activities that occur naturally in the home and community. Ideally, service providers and the family work collaboratively to promote the infant's health and development in ways that strengthen family functioning. Interventions that add to family stress and cannot be readily incorporated into daily routines are unlikely to produce desired outcomes.

The most important consideration in the design of home-visiting services is the needs of the infant and family. The reason the family has been referred for services is related to the special circumstances of the infant. These needs are typically numerous and might include medical, (e.g., gastrostomy tube, oxygen dependence, seizures, or cardiac condition), developmental (e.g., prematurity or cognitive limitations due to neurological damage), sensory (e.g., visual impairment or hearing loss), or motor (e.g., cerebral palsy or spina bifida). The infant with multiple disabilities may have a variety of service needs that occur in various combinations and levels and may warrant the involvement of more than one service provider or specialist. Similarly, families have various characteristics that interact in complex ways with the unique needs of their infants.

The particular characteristics of the infant, including nature and severity of the disability, health status, and temperament will influence the most appropriate kinds of interventions for any particular infant. A significant consideration in early intervention and working with families is the degree of difficulty and complexity of caring for the child (Bernheimer & Weisner, 2007). Thus, an infant who is medically fragile and technology dependent or who is chronically irritable and difficult to console might cause greater stress for the family than another infant who, though severely delayed, is in relatively good health and has an easygoing temperament. As a result of complex needs, some infant's signals may be considered "preintentional" because subtle or atypical intentional communication behaviors may be difficult for caregivers or professionals to interpret. The infant's apparent low level of responsiveness can have a significant impact upon caregiver-infant interaction and relationship.

Ideally, service providers and the family work collaboratively to promote the infant's health and development in ways that strengthen family functioning.

Another way in which the infant's characteristics impact service delivery is the number of professionals and agencies involved in providing early intervention. Families of infants with complex needs usually will receive services from more than one service provider. For example, an early interventionist trained in early childhood special education will likely provide family supports and design interventions to facilitate the child's development in all areas, whereas a physical therapist might focus on the child's motor skills. A service provider from any discipline should obtain accurate information regarding the infant's history and current status as well as about the other service providers involved with the family.

Family characteristics, including their values, family structure, cultural background, resources, and attitudes toward intervention and disability (Lynch & Hanson, 2004; Turnbull, Turnbull, Erwin, & Soodak, 2006), also will determine the specifics of a home-visiting approach. For example, the priorities and resources of parents with a large extended family and a network of other community supports might lead to a preference for home visits that focus on learning about their child's disability, accessing relevant research and Web sites, and gaining as much information as possible about different intervention services. On the other hand, a single mother who is new to the community and has limited social and financial resources may prefer a more relationship-based approach that focuses on providing both emotional and material supports for her as well as strengthening her relationship with her infant.

Early intervention services should be family centered and recognize that complex factors mediate family preferences.

Early intervention services should be family centered and should recognize that complex factors mediate family preferences and comfort levels with different in-home service delivery practices. As a family's circumstances change over time, so will their concerns and priorities related to early intervention services. The following vignettes will be used to demonstrate the components and variable characteristics of in-home service delivery design.

Carolina and Josie

Carolina is a 17-year-old single parent. She lives with her grandmother and 18-month-old daughter, Josie. Carolina describes Josie as "the most adorable baby ever" because she is very social and smiles a lot. In addition to her grandmother's Social Security, the family receives some public assistance. Prior to Josie's birth, Carolina attended high school and helped her grandmother with expenses by working in a local fast food restaurant. Carolina has not yet returned to school but hopes that she will be able to receive her high school diploma. Right after Josie was born, a friendly lady from an agency visited the family to explain about services for "special needs children." Carolina saw no reason to sign up for services, because Josie was healthy and happy and not having any problems. Initially she had some difficulty learning to take the bottle, but Carolina's grandmother helped her solve that problem. When Josie was born at the hospital, Carolina was told that Josie had Down syndrome. Carolina understood this to mean that "she would have certain features like almond-shaped eyes and short fingers." She doesn't recall receiving any other information about Down syndrome, and the nurses told her that the baby was very healthy. Carolina has recently discovered that Josie has a moderate hearing loss. When she took Josie to have her hearing tested, she was given information regarding how to obtain services for her. Carolina was again unsure just what these services might be.

The Garcias

Ron and Marilyn Garcia are both physicians. Ron is a plastic surgeon, and Marilyn is an endocrinologist. They are in their early 40s, have recently finished paying their medical school loans, and had been looking forward to building their dream home. They have an 8-year-old son, Ron Jr., and a 6-year-old daughter, Lilly. A year ago, Marilyn and Ron were upset when they discovered unexpectedly that Marilyn was pregnant. They quickly abandoned their initial considerations of terminating the pregnancy, influenced by their Catholic faith and Latino family background. Marilyn planned to work throughout the pregnancy and hoped to find a good live-in caregiver so she could return to her practice a couple of months after the baby's birth. The pregnancy was difficult, with Marilyn on bed rest during the last 2 months. Alex was delivered at 28 weeks gestation, weighing 2.5 pounds. He was placed on a respirator with multiple complications, including retinopathy of prematurity and respiratory distress syndrome. Despite their medical backgrounds, both Ron and Marilyn were stressed by these diagnoses and their older children were alarmed by their parents' concerns.

Delivery of Home-Visiting Services

An important variable in home-visiting practices for infants with multiple disabilities is that multiple service providers from different disciplines may be involved with the family. Families might be unsure of each person's role and discipline. They might be confused and frustrated by conflicting information. Ideally, the roles of each home visitor should be clearly defined and well coordinated within an interdisciplinary team model (Horn & Jones, 2004; McWilliam, 2005) and by an identified service coordinator. There is also variability in how service coordination is structured. In the dedicated model, the agency that employs service coordinators provides only service coordination. In the intra-agency model, the agency provides early intervention services and service coordination, whereas in the blended model, service coordinators provide both early intervention services and service coordination (Bruder & Dunst, 2008). In addition, the key roles played by family members and other caregivers (e.g., nannies, friends, neighbors) also should be understood.

Multiple service providers from different disciplines may be involved with the family.

Some home visitors have very specific therapeutic, direct-service roles and others provide consultation and interact with the family frequently. An early interventionist will take a more comprehensive view of the family, infant, and service delivery system in order to optimize the infant's development and the family's well-being. Some home visitors are paraprofessionals who work under the supervision of a therapist or early interventionist. Ideally, all service providers will be appropriately certified in their discipline and knowledgeable about additional community services. They will have an understanding of the interrelatedness of all developmental domains, as well as the importance of interdisciplinary collaboration and communication across disciplines. Service providers must work as members of a problem-solving team that includes family members as essential key players.

Josie's team of early intervention professionals included an early interventionist (i.e., Maxine), an educator in the deaf and hard-of-hearing area (DHH), and a speech language pathologist, each employed by different agencies. Both Carolina and her grandmother usually participated in home visits that were scheduled when they were available, even after Carolina returned to high school to complete her senior year. Maxine, the early interventionist from the local Part C program, was the primary service provider and service coordinator and made weekly home visits. The DHH educator and speech language pathologist were available as consultants regarding Josie's language and communication development. Once Josie received her hearing aids, the DHH educator helped Carolina and her grandmother learn how to care for and put them on Josie. The educator also demonstrated ways to encourage Josie's listening skill, (e.g., calling her name and making sure the TV was off so that she could hear them). The team also discussed the use of signs for key words to facilitate her language development. Carolina loved how Josie looked at her when she signed mama.

Alex's team of early intervention professionals included an early interventionist and an educator certified in visual impairments (VI) who worked for the same agency. Most of the time, they each made weekly home visits to the family, with a joint visit every couple of months. The service coordinator was employed by another agency and was involved mainly through IFSP meetings and other required contacts. In the first 6 months after Alex was released from the hospital, Ron arranged his schedule so he could participate in home visits. When Alex was 9 months old, they hired a nanny and Marilyn returned to work. Home visits were usually with the nanny, although once in a while either Ron or Marilyn would be home. Sometimes the older children joined the conversation when home visits were in the late afternoon. The Garcias were concerned mainly about ways to encourage Alex's development because of his vision loss. The VI educator modeled ways to encourage Alex's interest in people and things in the environment and motor development. The early interventionist helped the family and the nanny embed learning opportunities within Alex's daily activities.

The expertise of each discipline is critical in developing and providing high-quality early intervention services, even more so when an infant has multiple disabilities. For example, if the infant is deaf and has cerebral palsy, an educator certified in the areas of hearing loss and a physical therapist are essential members of the intervention team. The educator certified in hearing loss can assist the family in learning about the range of available communication options and amplification devices (e.g., sign language, speech, hearing aids, and cochlear implants) that are available for their child. Parents have to make a decision about which option to select for their child and learn to use that option effectively and consistently. The physical therapist should contribute information about the child's motor skills and how they may influence the child's ability to access communication (e.g., whether the child will be able to produce hand movements required for signing; positioning that will enable the child to visually attend to signed input).

It is essential to assist families with the communication and coordination of service providers, particularly when there are multiple service providers from different agencies. In some cases, the service coordinator

may assume these responsibilities. There are practical ways, however, to facilitate communication among service providers. For example, families may keep a binder of summary notes from each service provider, with photos or video samples that demonstrate selected interventions. Service providers could make joint visits as needed, plan face-to-face meetings, and maintain contact or share information through e-mail and other technology, as appropriate. These methods of communication are also invaluable ways to communicate with parents and other primary caregivers who may not be present during home visits.

Identify and Use Natural Learning Opportunities

A major emphasis of home-visiting services should be the infusion of interventions within the natural learning opportunities of the family's daily routines (Bernheimer & Weisner, 2007). Early interventionists promote positive relationships and enhance collaboration with families and caregivers through conversations about daily routines to identify natural learning opportunities. Dunst and colleagues have described the characteristics and significance of natural learning opportunities that occur in the everyday activity settings, or natural environments, in which families and their young children participate (Dunst, Bruder, Trivette, Hamby, Raab, & McLean, 2001a, 2001b; Dunst, Trivette, Humphries, Raab, & Roper, 2001; Raab & Dunst, 2004). Examples include a variety of daily home routines (e.g., bathing, getting dressed, and mealtimes) and community activities (e.g., going to the park, visiting relatives, and going to the grocery store). Furthermore, Dunst and colleagues (2001a, 2001b) found that learning opportunities that interest, engage, and motivate the infant promote the child's abilities through practice and exploration within everyday activities and are positively related to child progress. The number of activities in which the child and family participate is associated with increased child participation in learning opportunities and child outcomes (Dunst et al., 2001a).

A major emphasis of home-visiting services should be the infusion of interventions within the natural learning opportunities of the family's daily routines.

One of the first home-visit activities of the early interventionist might be to invite the parents to share a typical day in the life of their family, focusing on the infant's daily routines and identifying what is enjoyable and what is challenging for the infant and the family. In this way the early interventionist conveys that although he or she has certain professional expertise and experience, the parents' roles are foremost in the child's development, and family-professional collaboration is essential. Furthermore, professional recommendations are best applied within the framework of information and experience provided by the family, so this intertwining of family and early interventionist observations and sharing of information is integral to an effective intervention process.

Facilitate Caregiver-Infant Interaction

A significant goal of early intervention, regardless of the specific disability or discipline, is to support positive caregiver-infant interactions, because the quality of these early interactions can positively influence a child's learning and development across developmental domains (Keilty, 2008; McCollum, Gooler, Appl, & Yates, 2001). Research indicates that the caregiver-infant relationship is enhanced through interactions in which caregivers recognize, interpret, and respond to the infant's communicative intents and facilitate the child's efforts (Dunst & Kassow, 2004; Kassow & Dunst, 2004). When an infant has complex medical needs and multiple disabilities, early natural interactions with caregivers may be disrupted, for example, by the infant's frequent hospitalizations or subtle and atypical signals. Caregivers of these infants often appreciate specific ways to engage their babies in early interactions. The following strategies have been found to enhance caregiver interactions with infants who have complex and multiple needs (Chen, Klein, & Haney, 2007; Chen, Klein, & Minor, 2008).

Interpret the Infant's Signals. The service provider can ask the caregiver about the infant's behaviors and ways in which the infant expresses attention, interests, needs, and desires, as well as internal states such as pleasure or discomfort. For example, ask the caregiver about the infant's typical day and about the infant's facial expressions, vocalizations, body movements, and gestures and what these behaviors seem to indicate. When does the infant seem most alert? Together the caregiver and service provider should make systematic observations of the infant's behaviors and reactions during caregiving routines. In this way caregivers may identify, interpret, and respond to an infant's subtle, idiosyncratic, and sometimes puzzling signals. For example, initially it was difficult for Ron and Marilyn to figure out when Alex was paying attention or what he was noticing, due to his lack of eye contact or excited vocalization. Through suggestions from the educator certified in visual impairment, they discovered that Alex tended to be very quiet when he was paying attention and noticed that he moved his hands and fingers when he was interested in something.

Identify the Infant's Preferences. Once the infant's communicative and behavioral repertoire is recognized and understood, certain strategies can be used to identify the infant's likes and dislikes. This information can then be used to motivate the infant's interactions and increase communicative initiations. For example, the family can observe the infant's reactions to different toys, people, and activities. Does the baby respond to rough-and-tumble play with siblings? When is the child fussy? Who is a favorite person for the baby? Encourage siblings to help identify the infant's preferences. Siblings are frequently reliable sources of information and active participants in activities to find out what an infant likes and dislikes. A review of the infant's preferences may reveal particular characteristics of objects, activities, and even people that engage the child. For example, Carolina noticed that Josie liked toys with lights or moving parts, whereas Ron Jr. and Lilly found out that Alex loved toys that vibrated or made sounds. These preferred characteristics might be used to select toys and develop activities to promote a range of developmental skills, such as the infant's reaching, searching, or requesting behaviors. The infant's preferences can be used to elicit his or her initiations and to scaffold participation in less-liked activities. For example, an infant who enjoys the sound of singing (high preference) may be more cooperative during a disliked activity if the caregiver uses a song to encourage the infant's participation.

Establish Predictable Routines. Infants learn to make sense of the physical and social environment through repeated and predictable patterns of daily experience. Predictable routines also assist the caregiving process, particularly when the infant has medical needs (e.g., suctioning a tracheostomy or gastrostomy tube). Ask caregivers to identify frequently occurring activities that may be established in a consistent order each day. For example, what usually happens before and after breakfast, a diaper change, naptime, or going to the car? These predictable routines provide excellent natural opportunities for infusing discipline-specific interventions. For example, before feeding a baby who has low vision and hypotonia, the caregiver should position the infant in a padded adaptive chair to promote trunk control and reaching, then hold the bright yellow bottle within the infant's visual field and move it slowly side to side in front of the baby to obtain the child's visual attention and promote visual fixation and following.

Provide Anticipatory Cues. Once specific routines have been established, certain cues should be added to help infants develop a sense of

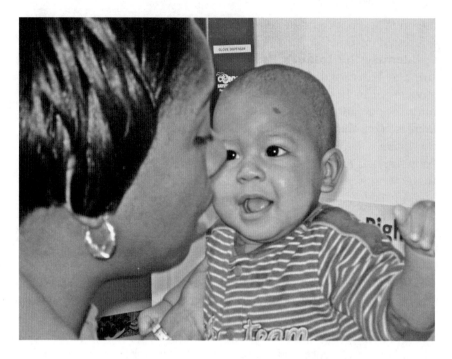

anticipation and confidence. *Cues* are the consistent use of certain words and sounds in addition to selected objects, visuals, or touches just before the activity. Cues should be associated with the activity to help the infant understand what they represent. For example, before taking the child to the highchair, show him a bib so that he knows it is time to eat, or before picking the child up from the high chair, say "Up, up, up" while touching the child under the arms and then pick up the child. Over time the child will demonstrate association between the sounds of the words and touch cue by raising his or her arms in anticipation of being picked up. The use of concrete cues is essential for infants who do not seem to understand speech, particularly if the child is visually inattentive, has a visual impairment, or has difficulty with transitions. Encourage caregivers to identify a few cues for the most frequent routines and to use them consistently. The identification and use of cues is another opportunity to involve siblings and other family members in supporting the infant's learning and development.

Ron Jr. and Lilly each identified different cues that they wanted to use with Alex in various situations (e.g., Ron Jr. wanted to give Alex a toy car whereas Lilly wanted to put Alex's hat on his head as cues for when the family was going out). In discussion with their parents, the children agreed to use the hat, Lilly's selected cue, for going out and that Ron Jr. could select the cue for another activity.

Develop Turn-Taking Games. Back-and-forth interactions between caregiver and infant are early conversations that promote the caregiver-infant relationship. For example, an infant babbles, mother waits for the infant to pause, then imitates the infant's vocalization and pauses for the infant to take a turn. When infants have significant disabilities, however, such turn-taking games may not develop without structuring specific opportunities based on the infant's behavioral repertoire and supporting the infant's response to take a turn. These games need to be mutually enjoyable and within the infant's abilities to motivate his or her active participation. For example, Lilly discovered that when she kisses Alex by nuzzling his cheek and making a loud smacking sound, he moves his head and smiles in excitement. She structures a turn-taking game by kissing Alex's other cheek to encourage his head movements and smiles, waiting for his response, and then kissing Alex again to extend the turn-taking game. Through this simple turn-taking activity, Lilly's confidence and interactions are reinforced by her baby brother's delight in the game, and Alex learns how to elicit his sister's contingent responsiveness and undivided attention.

Encourage Child's Communicative Initiations. Once the infant's favorite activities have been identified and occur consistently and predictably, the interruption and pause-and-wait strategies may be used to motivate the infant to initiate communication. For example, Josie loved playing a "giddyup horsey" game that involved being bounced on Carolina's knee. Maxine, the interventionist, encouraged (coached) Carolina to stop the bouncing and wait for some response from Josie (Klein, Chen, & Haney, 2000). At first Josie would only nod her head and Carolina would say, "OK more horsey, giddyup," and resume bouncing while saying, "Giddyup horsey, giddyup horsey." Through repeated opportunities, Josie began to vocalize. Over time her vocalizations were shaped into speech approximations: "Gi up!" Maxine expressed her pleasure at Josie's progress and commented on the great job Carolina was doing to help Josie with her speech and language development. Carolina began to think of ways to extend this procedure to other favorite activities. Maxine suggested trying to find ways to get Josie to initiate the request for the game before they started playing it. Maxine shared the success of this game with Josie's DHH consultant and the speech language pathologist. She also consulted with a physical therapist to see if the horsey game might be used to improve Josie's tone and postural stability.

This horsey game is an example of an activity that not only promoted social interaction between a mother and her child but also could be used to provide a natural opportunity for infusing discipline-specific interventions for the infant, that is, from speech and language (communication), physical therapy (sitting, balance, or postural control), and occupational therapy (level of arousal and sensory processing).

Change Over Time

The nature, frequency, and content of home-visiting services to a family and infant with multiple disabilities will change over time, given the bidirectional influence of contributing elements. For example, the child's developmental progress or changes in medical conditions may result in varied strategies or activities and different services to address current needs.

Once Alex's medical concerns were resolved and he was 2 years old, his parents asked the educator certified in VI how they could learn Braille and whether there were some parents of preschoolers who were blind whom they could meet.

Often, one of the most challenging examples of these changing needs occurs at the time of transition from highly supportive, family-centered early intervention in-home services to an educationally child-focused preschool classroom setting. Careful and timely preparation and anticipation of the transition processes (e.g., assessment, placement decisions, development of the individualized educational program) are crucial to the family and child's success during this time.

The nature, frequency, and content of home-visiting services to a family and infant with multiple disabilities will change over time.

As Josie approached 30 months of age, the point at which a transition IFSP meeting must be held to plan the transition from early intervention to preschool services, Carolina told Maxine that she and her grandmother wanted Josie to go to the local Head Start program because several children from the neighborhood went there. This discussion allowed ample time for Maxine and Carolina to think about what kinds of supports Josie would need in order to continue making good developmental progress and also be successfully included in a preschool with her friends.

Ultimately, the effectiveness of a particular configuration of home-visiting services may be evaluated by its goodness of fit with the infant's needs and the family's priorities, concerns, and resources during a *particular period of time.* All of the interventions described previously will be adapted, deleted, and reconfigured as the child's and family's circumstances and priorities change over time.

Conclusion

Home visits in early intervention should reflect evidence-based, family-centered, interdisciplinary practices. Evidence-based practices in early intervention are drawn from research, professional knowledge, and family wisdom (Buysee & Wesley, 2006a, 2006b). The conceptual framework for designing home-visiting early intervention services, presented in this article, is derived from the early intervention literature and professional expertise. The focus on caregiver-infant interactions and selected strategies is based on relevant early intervention research and professional and family experience. High-quality home-based early intervention services are characterized by family-professional collaboration to design interventions that address the family's priorities and concerns; fit natural learning opportunities within daily routines; and reflect a coordinated interdisciplinary approach to promote the infant's development and the family's confidence, competence, and delight in caring for their baby.

Note
You may contact Deborah Chen by email at deborah.chen@csun.edu

References
Bernheimer, L. P. & Weisner, T. S. (2007). "Let me just tell you what I do all day...": The family story at the center of intervention research and practice. *Infants & Young Children, 20,* 192-201.

Bruder, M. D. & Dunst, C. J. (2008). Factors related to the scope of early intervention coordinator practices. *Infants & Young Children, 21,* 176-185.

Buysse, V. & Wesley, P. W. (Eds.). (2006a). *Evidence-based practice in the early childhood field.* Washington, DC: Zero to Three Press.

Buysse, V. & Wesley, P. W. (2006b). Making sense of evidence-based practice: Reflections and recommendations. In V. Buysee & P. W. Wesley (Eds.), *Evidence-based practice in the early childhood field* (pp. 227-246). Washington, DC: Zero to Three Press.

Chen, D., Klein, M. D., & Haney, M. (2007). Promoting interactions with infants who have complex multiple disabilities: Development and field-testing of the PLAI curriculum. *Infants & Young Children, 20,* 149-162.

Chen, D., Klein, M. D., & Minor, L. (2008). Online professional development for early interventionists. Learning a systematic approach to promote caregiver interactions with infants who have multiple disabilities. *Infants & Young Children, 21,* 120-133.

Dunst, C. J., Bruder, M. B., Trivette, C. M., Hamby, D., Raab, M., & McLean, M. (2001a). Characteristics and consequences of everyday learning opportunities. *Topics in Early Childhood Special Education, 21,* 68-92.

Dunst, C. J., Bruder, M. B., Trivette, C. M., Hamby, D, Raab, M., & McLean, M. (2001b). Natural learning opportunities for infants, toddlers, and preschoolers. *Young Exceptional Children, 4*(3), 18-25.

Dunst, C. J. & Kassow, D. Z. (2004). Characteristics of interventions promoting parental sensitivity to child behavior. *Bridges, 2*(5), 1-17. Retrieved February 15, 2008, from http://www.researchtopractice.info/bridges/bridges_vol2_no5.pdf

Dunst, C. J., Trivette, C. M., Humphries, T., Raab, M., & Roper, N. (2001). Contrasting approaches to natural learning environment interventions. *Infants & Young Children,14*(2), 48-63.

Horn, E. M., & Jones, H. (2004). Collaborating and teaming in early intervention and early childhood special education. In Horn, E. M., Ostrosky, M. M., & Jones, H. (Eds). Interdisciplinary teams. *Young Exceptional Children Monograph Series, No. 6, Interdisciplinary teams* (pp. 11-20). Longmont, CO: Sopris West.

Jung, L. A. (2007). Writing individualized family plan strategies that fit into the routine. *Young Exceptional Children, 10*(3), 2-9.

Kassow, D. Z. & Dunst, C. J. (2004). Relationship between parental contingent-responsiveness and attachment outcomes. *Bridges, 2*(4), 1-17. Retrieved February 19, 2008, from http://www.researchtopractice.info/bridges/bridges_vol2_no4.pdf

Keilty, B. (2008). Early intervention home-visiting principles in practice: A reflective approach. *Young Exceptional Children, 11*(2), 29-40.

Klein, M. D. (in press). Home visiting approaches in early intervention serving infants with disabilities. In D. Chen (Ed.), *Early intervention in action. Working across disciplines to support infants with multiple disabilities and their families* [CD-ROM]. Baltimore: Brookes.

Klein, M. D., Chen, D., & Haney, M. (2000). *Promoting learning through active interaction. A guide to early communication with young children who have multiple disabilities.* Baltimore: Brookes.

Lynch, E. W. & Hanson, M. J. (2004). *Developing cross-cultural competence. A guide for working with children and their families.* Baltimore: Brookes.

McCollum, J. A., Gooler, F. G., Appl, D. J., & Yates, T. J. (2001). PIWI: Enhancing parent-child interaction as a foundation for early intervention. *Infants & Young Children, 14*(1), 34-45.

McWilliam, R. A. (2005). DEC recommended practices: Interdisciplinary models. In S. Sandall, M. L. Hemmeter, B. J. Smith, & M. McLean (Eds.), *DEC recommended practices. A comprehensive guide for practical application in early intervention/early childhood special education* (pp. 127-146). Longmont, CO: Sopris West.

Raab, M. & Dunst, C. J. (2004). Early intervention practitioner approaches to natural environment interventions. *Journal of Early Intervention, 27,* 15-26.

Raab, M. & Dunst, C. J. (2006). Influence of child interests on variations in child behavior and functioning. *Bridges,4*(2), 1-22. Retrieved February 15, 2008, from http://www.researchtopractice.info/bridges/bridges_vol4_no2.pdf

Sandall, S., Hemmeter, M. L., Smith, B. J., & McLean, M. E. (2005). *DEC recommended practices. A comprehensive guide for practical application in early intervention/early childhood special education.* Longmont, CO: Sopris West.

Turnbull, A., Turnbull, R., Erwin, E., & Soodak, L. (2006). *Families, professionals and exceptionality: Positive outcomes through partnerships and trust* (5th ed.). Upper Saddle River, NJ: Prentice Hall.

Inclusive Playgroups: Supporting the Development of Infants and Toddlers

Mary-alayne Hughes, Ph.D.

LaShorage Shaffer, Ed.M.

Hasan Y. Zaghlawan, M.S.
University of Illinois at Urbana–Champaign

O n a cold, snowy Saturday morning in February, 10 toddlers are enjoy-ing the attention of their parents. The sound of clatter and voices fills a room arranged with several play areas, including a mat with blocks of various sizes, shapes, and textures; a play kitchen with empty food boxes, toy cash registers, and toy grocery carts; and a book corner with puppets and stuffed animals. There is even a "messy" table that is covered with drawing paper and finger paints mixed with shav-ing cream. The toddlers are scattered throughout the room playing with their parents. Two-and-a-half-year-old Jarron makes car noises as he moves a blue and red car on the mat. His mother is sitting on the carpet with a yellow car and talking about what she and Jarron are doing as they play with the cars. Victoria, 18 months old, is sit-ting in her dad's lap in the book corner as he reads The Very Hungry Caterpillar. She holds a caterpillar puppet as he reads to her and two other children who are interested in the story. These families are par-ticipating in a Saturday morning playgroup. What is interesting about this playgroup is that many of the children have developmental delays, and their participation in a playgroup is one of the activities on their Individualized Family Service Plans (IFSPs).

Young children learn about the world through play. Initially, play takes the form of simple games and turn-taking routines (e.g., peekaboo). As children grow and develop, their play expands and becomes more com-plex through interactions with the people and objects in their environ-ment. Within this context, parents are their child's first play partners and teachers. They have individualized knowledge about their child's pref-erences, interests, and routines. In addition, there is a wealth of infor-mation on development and learning that is available through books, magazines, videos, television programs, and the Internet. However, though numerous sources of information are readily available, understanding how to use the information to facilitate development and learning can be challenging for many parents, especially first-time parents. Parents of children with delays or disabilities may face additional challenges. For example, some children with disabilities have delayed communication and motor abilities that may make interaction and play challenging. Some parents may have difficulty reading their child's cues or may misread their child's attempts at social interaction and play.

Young children learn about the world through play.

Participating in parent-child playgroups is an effective way for parents to learn more about play and how to use it to facilitate development and learning. Research has shown that stimulating play environments enhance cognition throughout childhood (Stegelin, 2005), and active adult involvement can increase the social level of play and beneficially impact cognitive growth (Ward, 1996). Parents can learn new and effective strategies for supporting their child's development if they understand the importance of play and their role as play partners. When parents understand the impact they have on development and how playing with their child can support that development, they are more likely to engage in activities that enhance their child's development and growth (Kaiser & Hancock, 2003). They also will understand that "children are never just playing" (Wilford, 2005, p. 19).

Over the last decade, embedding intervention within natural environments has been emphasized within the early intervention field (Sandall, Hemmeter, Smith, & McLean, 2005) and was codified in the 1997 reauthorization and reaffirmed in the 2004 reauthorization of the Individuals with Disabilities Education Act (IDEA). Initially, as new policies about natural environments were implemented, early interventionists tended to narrowly interpret the term as a location or setting. More recently, researchers have supported a much broader conceptualization: "Natural learning environments are the everyday experiences, events, and places that are sources of children's learning opportunities" (Dunst, Bruder, Trivette, Raab, & McLean, 2001, p. 18). Within these natural opportunities, learning may occur serendipitously, or learning activities may be purposefully planned (Dunst et al.).

A child's home is a natural context for learning, providing numerous opportunities for learning within daily routines. In early intervention, home visits often constitute a primary means for service delivery. However, Dunst, Bruder, Trivette, and Hamby, et al. (2001) emphasized that numerous learning opportunities outside of the home also are natural contexts for services. From this ecological perspective, playgroups are an example of a normative activity for all young children and families, serving as a source of both serendipitous and planned learning opportunities.

Playgroups can be designed in a variety of ways for a variety of purposes. For example, some community playgroups are drop-off programs in which the child participates without the parent, or the parent stays and observes the playgroup from the sidelines. Typically, the focus is peer socialization. Other playgroups are structured so that the children play together (peer socialization) while the parents meet separately for the purposes of networking and support. For playgroups to be used effectively as an intervention, however, the structure and process should be supported by research and recommended practices. Parents interacting with infants (PIWI) is an example of an evidence-based intervention model. It is not a commercial curriculum or product. Rather, it is a *framework* or model that can be applied in a variety of environments, including homes, playgroups, and other natural learning contexts. The foundation of this framework is the philosophy that infant/toddler development and learning occurs within the context of relationships, and the most important relationship is the one between the primary caregiver (hereafter referred to as the parent) and child. The interventionist's role is to *facilitate* parent-child interaction by using a variety of strategies designed to encourage interaction. For both parents and children, key outcomes include an increased sense of competence, confidence, and mutually pleasurable interactions (McCollum, Yates, & Gooler, 1999).

Natural learning environments are the everyday experiences, events, and places that are sources of children's learning opportunities.

With this relationship-based philosophy as the foundation, there are seven additional components that serve as building blocks for the PIWI model, which is presented in Figure 1: environments, planning, individualizing, facilitator team (interventionists), triadic relationships, developmental topics, and dyadic relationships (McCollum et al., 1999). The primary focus is the dyadic relationship between the parent and child, which is represented by the top block. The other building blocks scaffold this primary dyadic relationship.

The purpose of this article is to describe the use of the PIWI model within the structure of an inclusive playgroup. The purpose of the play-

Figure 1
PIWI Building Blocks

From McCollum et al. (1999). *PIWI Projects: A Relationship-Based Approach to Early Intervention. A Training Curriculum for Early Intervention Personnel, Birth-3.* Reprinted with permission from the authors.

group is threefold: (1) to provide parents with ideas for promoting their child's development; (2) to facilitate opportunities for parent-child play and interaction; and (3) to encourage parent networking and support. For children with delays or disabilities, opportunities to address IFSP outcomes are embedded within the play activities during each playgroup session.

Although playgroups are a natural environment for infants as well as toddlers, this article specifically focuses on the use of an inclusive (i.e., enrolling toddlers with and without developmental delays) playgroup for toddlers. In particular, the discussion will embed the PIWI building blocks across the three phases of early intervention services: planning, implementation, and evaluation. Additional discussion about specific components of the model can be found in McCollum and Yates (1994); McCollum, Yates, Gooler, and Bruns (2001); and McCollum et al. (1999).

Playgroup Planning

Planning is a critical feature of implementing an inclusive toddler playgroup as an intervention tool. Critical aspects of the planning phase include logistical arrangements, participant recruitment, and individual session planning.

Playgroups can be held in many different types of community facilities and locations, including recreation centers, playgrounds, church meeting rooms, community centers, child care centers, and preschool classrooms. Issues to consider when selecting a facility and location include the number of playgroup participants, accessibility, parking, and the extent to which playgroup participants will feel comfortable in the chosen setting.

The next step is to recruit families of children, with and without disabilities, to participate in the playgroup. There are many ways to disseminate recruitment information, including print (e.g., brochures, flyers), media (e.g., TV, radio), and electronic sources (e.g., Web sites, electronic mailing lists). The key is to disseminate the information as widely as possible and to have one person serve as point of contact for interested families.

Posting flyers in public and private community agencies, hospitals, and schools is a simple way to disseminate information. If the playgroup is held during consistent time periods throughout the year, then word-of-mouth communication also can be effective. Another avenue for dissemination is through the early intervention local coordinating council (LIC). An LIC is typically composed of representatives from a wide variety of public and private agencies that serve families of children ages birth to 5, and flyers can be disseminated at LIC meetings and through their Internet mailing lists.

Planning is a critical feature of implementing an inclusive toddler playgroup as an intervention tool.

One recruitment challenge is attracting the families of toddlers with or at-risk for delays or disabilities. Although some children in this age group are more easily identified for services at an early age (e.g., Down syndrome, speech/language delays, physical disability), many delays or disabilities often are not identified until the child is in preschool or early elementary grades. Even if the child is identified early, some parents may be reluctant to participate in a playgroup with typically developing children for a variety of reasons. Health issues may be a concern for some parents. For example, a child may be medically fragile or simply more prone to illness, making the parent reluctant to participate in any type of group activity. Parents also may be struggling with their own thoughts and feelings about their child's delays. Appl, Fahl-Gooler, and McCollum (1997) retrospectively interviewed parents who had participated in an inclusive playgroup. Their results showed that some parents reported difficulty in participating, because it heightened their sensitivity to the differences between their child and the typically

developing children in the playgroup. However, in spite of this difficulty, many parents continued their participation, because their comfort level increased as they felt accepted and supported by the other parents and the playgroup facilitators. A strategy for easing families' concerns is to recruit local early interventionists to help disseminate information about the playgroup by distributing flyers and talking with families during home visits. The early interventionist has a relationship with the family and is viewed as a credible and trusted source of information. She or he can talk about the benefits of the playgroup, provide examples of the developmental topics, and explain how the child's IFSP outcomes can be addressed within the naturalistic social context of the playgroup sessions. Families also can be given the option to "try it out" to help ease any initial anxiety about their participation.

The next step in this process is to plan thoughtfully for each individual playgroup session. The PIWI model emphasizes the recommended practice of an interdisciplinary team approach (McWilliam, 2005), and the facilitator team (*PIWI building block*) is composed of interventionists from a variety of disciplines including but not limited to education, speech/language pathology, and occupational therapy. Major benefits of a team approach include the opportunity to holistically integrate intervention and to reduce fragmentation and duplication of services, whereas the challenges include finding time for planning and coordination. One way to address this challenge is to incorporate planning time into the team debriefing at the end of each playgroup session. After parents and children have departed, allow 20 to 30 minutes to clean up, discuss observations, document IFSP progress, and select the developmental topic for the next playgroup session. If there is time remaining, the facilitator team can plan for the next session. If not, the team can continue planning by using e-mail or some other form of computer technology (e.g., shared folder on a computer server).

During intervention planning (*PIWI building block*), the facilitator team incorporates three additional PIWI building blocks: environments, individualizing, and developmental topics. These components are reflected in two playgroup planning forms. The first planning form (presented in Table 1) contains information about the environment, group activities and strategies, individual intervention strategies for specific children, and team roles.

This form functions as a holistic lesson plan and helps structure the planning process. For example, the facilitator team gathers and uses a myriad of information (i.e., knowledge of child development, parent goals and concerns, parent and child interests, and IFSP outcomes) to individualize (*PIWI building block*) the process, including planning adaptations and modifications that support each child's functional participation. Moreover, individualizing for typically developing children is just as important as individualizing for children who are at risk for or have delays or disabilities. Activities are designed so that all of the parents and children have the opportunity to participate in some way. For example, during water-table play, there will need to be accommodations for a child who is in a wheelchair so that he or she can join in and reach the water.

Table 1
Playgroup Planning Form Template

	Environment (space/ materials)	Group activities and strategies	Individual strategies	Team roles
Greeting and hello song				
Opening discussion (DOT)				
Parent and child play activities				
Snack				
Songs and games				
Closing discussion (DOT) and goodbye song				

Note. DOT = developmental observation topic. From McCollum et al. (1999). *PIWI Projects: A Relationship-Based Approach to Early Intervention. A Training Curriculum for Early Intervention Personnel, Birth-3.* Adapted with permission from the authors.

A typically developing child who may be shorter than the other children may need a small stool to stand on so that he or she can reach into the water.

Individualizing and planning the play activities includes thoughtful consideration of the environment (e.g., space, materials, schedule). The environment (*PIWI building block*) is included on the planning form as a reminder to arrange the environment proactively. For example, certain types of toys (e.g., balls, blocks, sensory table) more easily promote interaction than others (e.g., pull toy). Rather than expensive commercial toys, toddlers are typically more interested in simple materials and objects that can be found in their home environment (e.g., plastic measuring cups, plastic containers, pots and pans, cardboard boxes). Using these types of materials during the playgroup sessions also shows parents that it is not necessary to purchase a commercial toy to play and have fun.

Activities are designed so that all of the parents and children have the opportunity to participate in some way.

One crucial aspect of the environment that is often overlooked is space. It helps to draw simple floor plans as a way to think about how to use the space effectively, including the location of different play areas, placement of furniture, placement of play materials, and "traffic flow" between the play areas. The amount of materials in the space is also a consideration. Too many materials may be overwhelming, but not enough materials also may be ineffective. Novelty facilitates interaction, and moving materials in and out of the room is another environmental strategy to consider.

In addition to environmental considerations, effective planning includes gathering information about each child's strengths, preferences, and interests, as well as the parents' concerns and goals for their child. There are several ways to accomplish this important task. First, information can be gathered during a home visit through informal conversation about the child's interests, daily routines, and favorite activities. It also is important to ask parents about their priorities and concerns and to be sensitive to potential cultural differences or preferences. This home visit provides insights about (1) the families' child-rearing values and practices; (2) the child's interactions in a familiar setting with parents, siblings, and other household members; and (3) the parents' concerns and goals for their child, including strategies and outcomes on the IFSP for those children receiving early intervention services. As the information is gathered, it can be organized into a summary matrix so that important information about each child and family is readily available to the facilitator team. A second way to gather information is to use a simple feedback form at the end of each playgroup session. Parents can be encouraged to provide (1) additional information about their priorities, concerns, and preferences and (2)  feedback about the session and future topics of interest. Giving parents an opportunity to provide feedback also demonstrates respect for their knowledge about their child and the important role they play as part of the intervention team.

The PIWI model uses child development as an organizing theme, with a developmental topic (*PIWI building block*) as the focus for each playgroup session. This developmental focus is reflected in the second playgroup planning form, referred to as the developmental observation topic (DOT). The facilitator uses the DOT plan to help structure the opening and closing discussions. In particular, the DOT helps focus parents' attention on a particular aspect of development, and it also provides the context for individual parents to observe and interact with their child. McCollum et al. (2001) provide detailed explanations and examples of both playgroup planning forms. Table 2 presents an example of the DOT.

Playgroup Implementation

There is flexibility in the number of playgroup sessions and in the length of each session; however, the duration of a typical PIWI toddler playgroup session is approximately 90 minutes once a week. The playgroups typically are conducted across a period of 6 to 8 weeks. Establishing a consistent routine and an engaging, safe environment is important for all of the families. The components and sequence of a playgroup session include the following: greeting and hello song (10 minutes), opening discussion (15 minutes), parent-and-child play (30 minutes), snack and conversation (15 minutes), songs and games (5 minutes), and closing discussion and goodbye song (15 minutes).

Prior to each playgroup session, it is important to ensure that the room is arranged and the materials are ready so that families who arrive early feel welcomed and engaged. Posters with short descriptions or

Table 2

Developmental Observation Topic (DOT) Plan for Ages 10 to 30 Months

Observation topic: How I explore my environment	Observation focus: What materials keep me interested and engaged?
Environment(s)	**Things to try**
Variety of types of objects and activities (large, small; familiar, unfamiliar; small/gross motor; water play; etc.), box with puppets and vehicles, tube box with balls and bean bags, sock box, wooden stairs with streamers, water table, puzzles, blocks and trucks	1. Wait and watch to see how your child explores the materials 2. Imitate your child's actions 3. Add a new object 4. Talk about what your child is doing 5. Watch to see what types of materials are interesting to your child
Opening discussion	**Closing discussion**
Introduction: Children are motivated to explore and conquer (objects and people). Different children explore in different ways and they explore differently when different types of objects are available and when they are comfortable in the situation. By watching what children do and what they practice over and over, we can get a good idea of what they are trying to learn and do. *Questions:* When are your children most active? What do they find most motivating? What keeps them playing for long periods of time? What happens when you add a new angle (object, action) to your child's play? *Predictions:* What materials will your child be most interested in? What will he/she be doing? In which area will your child spend the most time? *Main points:* When appropriate opportunities for exploring and learning are available, and when the situation is comfortable, children usually remain focused and engaged (point out examples using what children are doing during the discussion). Different children are motivated by different types of objects. Adults can help keep children interested by helping them extend what they are doing.	*Predictions:* Were you surprised by where and how long your children played? What went as expected? What didn't? *Questions:* What influenced the amount of time that children spent in one area (novelty of materials, challenging materials, parent strategies)? What strategies did you try to extend your child's play? What worked? *Carryover:* What materials does your child most enjoy at home? What materials do you have at home that you could use to help extend his/her play? What strategies might you try at home to help extend your child's play? *Main points:* When children are not challenged or are challenged too much, they tend to wander in their play. Different children explore differently, and enjoy different kinds of objects. Preferred objects and activities keep children engaged for longer periods than nonpreferred ones. Children need a stimulating and moderately challenging environment to foster exploration and engagement. Parents can help keep their children interested and channel their high energy level.

Note. From "Using 'DOTs' to Support Parents as Developmental Observers During Parent-Child Groups," by J. A. McCollum, T. J. Yates, F. Gooler, and D. Bruns, 2001, *Young Exceptional Children, Monograph Series No. 3, Teaching strategies: What to do to support young children's development* (p. 6). Longmont, CO: Sopris West. Copyright 2001 by the Division for Early Childhood. Reprinted with permission.

pictures of the playgroup activities can be hung around the room so that families who arrive late can join in without feeling awkward. As families arrive, they are warmly greeted by name, and recorded music (e.g., children's songs, lullabies) is played softly in the background to create an inviting atmosphere. A hello song signals the beginning of the playgroup session, and it is important that the song incorporates each person's first name. Young children love to hear their names! Repeating the same song each week elicits their attention and provides continuity and predictability, which is especially crucial for children with delays or disabilities.

The next component of the playgroup is the DOT opening discussion. When two or more interventionists constitute the facilitator team, it is helpful to divide the roles. Typically, one interventionist facilitates the parent discussion and the other engages the children with toys and materials that have been selected for this purpose. This same strategy also works well for the closing discussion. If only one interventionist is available to facilitate the playgroup, realistic consideration should be given to the number of families who are recruited to participate. Moreover, it becomes especially important to have novel toys and materials readily available in order to sustain the toddlers' attention while their parents participate in the opening and closing discussions. The following vignette illustrates an opening discussion with one facilitator.

Parents and children sit in a circle on the carpet as the hello song is sung. When the song is finished, the facilitator places a few new toys and play materials in the middle of the carpet as the children squeal with delight. The parents remain seated around the edges of the carpet, encircling the children. The facilitator begins the opening discussion about the developmental topic on communication and language, and she discusses the variety of play materials and activities that are arranged around the room. Victoria brings a toy over to her dad and then sits in his lap as he talks about her play interests and predicts which activity she might prefer. Jarron picks up a doll and wanders outside of the circle toward a toy highchair and play kitchen. Jarron's mother keeps an eye on him, dividing her attention between Jarron and the opening discussion. Two other toddlers are tugging at one of the puzzles, each wanting to play with the same puzzle. The facilitator redirects one of the toddlers with another puzzle while she listens to Jarron's mother talk about his play interests and her concerns about his language difficulties. As the discussion continues, another toddler begins to cry and his mother scoops him up in her arms and takes him to the rocker in the "quiet corner" where she can soothe him and continue to listen to the discussion. With toddlers, the environment is often noisy and busy; however, adults quickly learn to master the art of multitasking!

The most important aspect of the opening discussion is to talk about the DOT. It is helpful to point out the various toys, materials, and activities available in different play areas around the room and to describe how these are connected with the DOT for that session. In addition, the facilitator provides information about development in a manner that helps the parents make connections between the information and their child's development and learning. The most critical aspect of the opening discussion happens next: Parents are asked to *predict* what their child will be interested in and what activities they might try. This prediction is not used to gauge how well parents know their child, and there

> *The facilitator provides information about development in a manner that helps the parents make connections between the information and their child's development and learning.*

are no right or wrong answers. Rather, prediction is used as a strategy because it inherently facilitates observation. If parents have predicted what they think their child will do or enjoy, then they will probably watch and observe to see what actually happens. That observation then serves as a stepping stone for interaction. During this opening discussion, the parents' predictions are written on chart paper so they can be revisited during the closing discussion.

The pacing and length of the opening discussion will depend on the extent to which the parents feel comfortable participating in the discussion and the extent to which the children stay engaged with the toys and materials that have been spread out for this purpose. The opening discussion is concluded by briefly summarizing the main discussion points. As with the hello song, it's important to establish a signal for moving from the opening discussion to the play activities. It can be a simple announcement (e.g., "Let's go play!") or a slightly more elaborate signal (e.g., action song or dance movement). The important feature is that it is used consistently across the sessions. After the first few playgroups, starting the session and facilitating the opening discussion becomes easier as the playgroup routine becomes familiar.

The most important component of the each playgroup session is the opportunity for parent and child interaction, so parent-child play activities constitute a major portion of each session. Having purposefully arranged the play environment and thoughtfully selected the materials and activities ahead of time, now the interventionist's role is to facilitate parent-child interaction by using a variety of strategies designed to encourage interaction. In the PIWI model, the strategies are referred to as *triadic strategies* because there are three people involved: child, parent, and early interventionist (Figure 2).

Figure 2
Intervention Triad

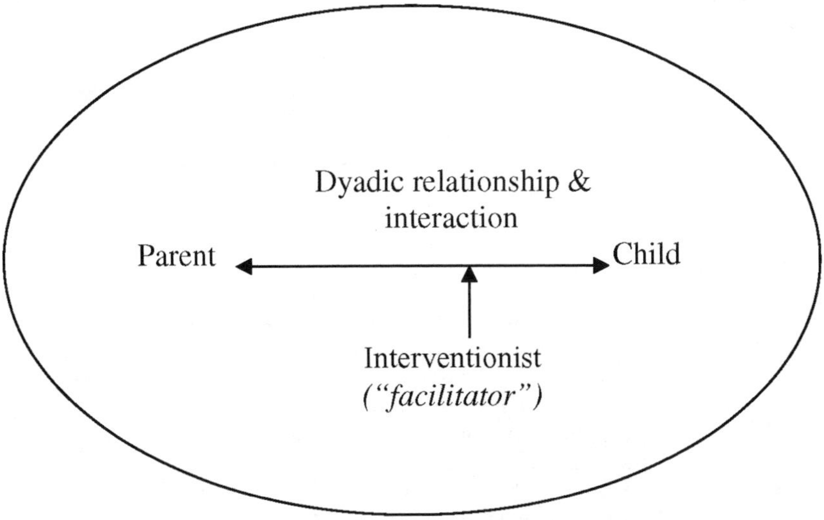

From McCollum et al. (1999). *PIWI Projects: A Relationship-Based Approach to Early Intervention. A Training Curriculum for Early Intervention Personnel, Birth-3.* Adapted with permission from the authors.

The facilitator team uses these strategies to build, expand, and reinforce parent-child interactions that are supportive of the child's development while also recognizing and strengthening the natural competence of the parent (McCollum et al., 1999). Table 3 briefly outlines these triadic strategies. Further explanation and details are provided in McCollum and Yates (1994).

Although the focus of the PIWI model is the parent-child interaction, an additional benefit of an inclusive playgroup is the opportunity for peer interaction and socialization. For many toddlers with delays or disabilities, this may be one of the few opportunities to participate in a group with typically developing peers. These peers are natural language models, and their curiosity and playfulness often create opportunities for proximity and engagement. The facilitator team can structure the environment to scaffold these naturally occurring opportunities for peer

Table 3
PIWI Triadic Strategies

Triadic strategy	Description	Example
Establish dyadic context	Environment is arranged to increase the probability of developmentally matched and mutually enjoyable parent-child interaction and play	Facilitator positions child where parent can see what the child is doing
Affirm parent competence	Developmentally supportive interactions are warmly recognized and expanded	Facilitator says, "Look at his big smile. He really likes to play with you like that."
Focus attention	Aspects of the interaction are commented upon, expanded, or questioned to draw the parent's attention to particular actions or competencies in self or child	Facilitator talks indirectly to the parent through the child saying, "I'm trying to figure out how this ball fits into this hole in the box."
Provide developmental information	Information about the child's development is given by verbally labeling or interpreting the child's emotional, cognitive, language, and/or motor abilities within the context of play and interactions	Facilitator explains to parent how to use an object or toy to encourage child to reach
Model	Dyadic interaction is modeled by the facilitator	Facilitator establishes a turn-taking routine with the child and then says, "Dad wants to play now."
Suggest	Facilitator provides parent with a suggestion to try with the child	Facilitator says, "I wonder what might happen if you stacked the blocks."

Note. From McCollum et al. (1999). *PIWI Projects: A Relationship-Based Approach to Early Intervention. A Training Curriculum for Early Intervention Personnel, Birth-3.* Adapted with permission from the authors.

interaction. In addition, parents often serendipitously facilitate peer interaction as they play with their own child and another child in the same play area.

As the parent-child play winds down, families and children transition to the snack area. Blowing bubbles is a great way to facilitate this transition, because toddlers never seem to tire of popping bubbles and they will follow the bubbles anywhere! Snack is served family style, which encourages children and families to interact. Parents often use this time to talk with each other and share informal resources about child health and development, nutrition, and parent resources within the local community. In addition, the facilitator team can use this time as a natural opportunity to talk about daily routines (e.g., meals) and child-rearing practices to address feeding concerns, as well as to model ways for parents to facilitate child language and communication.

Songs and games are used as a transition between snack and the closing discussion. Songs that require some type of action and movement are very engaging. Toddlers also love repetition, so it is helpful to sing numerous verses or compose additional verses for familiar songs. Songs and games also are learning tools that reinforce basic concepts and language. Parents are invited to share their child's favorite songs and games with the group, and these often become part of the playgroup routine from session to session. To transition to the closing discussion, several sedentary songs or games are used (e.g., lullabies, finger plays). Then, several new play materials can be brought into the room to engage the children during the closing discussion with the parents. The DOT is reviewed, and parents are encouraged to review their predictions and share observations about their child. This discussion provides a natural opportunity for the facilitator to reinforce and expand upon the parents' understanding of the DOT and other topics that may arise. At the end of the discussion, parents are

asked for ideas about future topics, activities, and materials. This often facilitates additional discussion about their concerns, priorities, and interests. Parents also appreciate receiving a written handout with ideas that can be implemented at home, including activities, songs, resources, and tips about development (e.g., Web sites, books, videos).

Playgroup Evaluation

To document each child's progress and to prepare for upcoming playgroup sessions, some form of evaluation should take place. One way to evaluate each playgroup session is to ask parents for feedback. Using a written feedback form that parents complete before they leave is an easy way to accomplish this task. It is important to keep it short and simple. For example, the form may include two or three questions about the specific activities and materials that were used during that session and additional space can be left for comments and suggestions about future developmental topics.

It also is helpful for the facilitator team to debrief and evaluate the session after parents and children have departed. The planning form can be used to guide the reflection about each segment of the playgroup, from arrival to departure. The focus is to identify what went well and what should be done differently for the next playgroup. Guiding questions often include the following: How effective was the opening discussion? Were parents engaged? Were the parent-child interaction activities developmentally appropriate for the children? Did the activities and materials capture the attention of the children and parents? Which triadic strategies worked well with which families? What modifications could have been made for a more successful and engaging playgroup session? This debriefing time provides an opportunity to reflect, discuss, and record observations. This documentation is used for progress

Using a playgroup for intervention requires thoughtful planning and an underlying philosophy that values the primacy of the parent-child relationship.

monitoring (including IFSP outcomes) and for planning the next playgroup session. In particular, this information can be used by the facilitator team to inform its planning and intervention for those families who may be receiving additional early intervention services through individual home visits. For example, one of Jarron's IFSP outcomes is to use words to communicate his wants and needs. After reading his IFSP, one of the playgroup facilitators consults with Jarron's mother and his early interventionist so that the vocabulary and strategies listed on the IFSP can be embedded into the playgroup activities. During opportunities to interact with Jarron and his mother in the playgroup, the facilitators record and tally Jarron's single-word utterances. After the goodbye song, they share their observations with Jarron's mother, which gives her an opportunity to add her own observations. One of the facilitators summarizes this information in an e-mail that is sent to Jarron's mother and Jarron's early interventionist.

Summary

Inclusive playgroups inherently provide natural learning opportunities for toddlers and their families. In addition, if grounded in an intervention model that reflects recommended practice, playgroups can be effective means for implementing early intervention services. However, using a playgroup for intervention requires thoughtful planning and an underlying philosophy that values the primacy of the parent-child relationship. These features are exemplified in the PIWI model. PIWI acknowledges parent competence and facilitates parents' confidence in supporting their child's development. Planning is individualized, the environment is purposefully arranged, and the interventionist uses triadic strategies to facilitate positive and mutually pleasurable dyadic interactions.

When inclusive playgroups are used as a vehicle for intervention, there is more there than meets the eye. For Jarron and Victoria in the opening vignette, the inclusive playgroup provides opportunities to address their IFSP goals in a way that is interesting, engaging and just plain fun!

Note
You may contact Mary-Alayne Hughes by email at mahughes@illinois.edu

References
Appl, D. J., Fahl-Gooler, F., & McCollum, J. A. (1997). Inclusive parent-child play groups: How comfortable are parents of children with disabilities in the groups? *Infant Toddler Intervention, 7,* 235-249.
Dunst, C. J., Bruder, M. B., Trivette, C. M., Hamby, D., Raab, M., & McLean, M. (2001). Characteristics and consequences of everyday natural learning opportunities. *Topics in Early Childhood Special Education, 21,* 68-92.
Dunst, C. J., Bruder, M. B., Trivette, C. M., Raab, M., & McLean, M. (2001). Natural learning opportunities for infants, toddlers, and preschoolers. *Young Exceptional Children, 4*(3), 18-25.
Individuals With Disabilities Education Improvement Act of 2004, Pub. L. No. 108-446, U.S.C. $1400.
Kaiser, A. P. & Hancock, T. B. (2003). Teaching parents new skills to support their young children's development. *Infants & Young Children, 16,* 9-21.
McCollum, J. A. & Yates, T. J. (1994). Dyad as focus, triad as means: A family-centered approach to supporting parent-child interactions. *Infants & Young Children, 6,* 54-63.
McCollum, J. A., Yates, T. J., & Gooler, F. (1999). *PIWI projects: A relationship-based approach to early intervention. A training curriculum for early intervention personnel (birth – 3).* (Available from University of Illinois Early Childhood Projects, Children's Research Center, 51 Gerty Drive, Champaign, IL 61820).

McCollum, J. A., Yates, T. J., Gooler, F., & Bruns, D. (2001). Using "DOTs" to support parents as developmental observers during parent-child groups. In M. Ostrosky & S. Sandall (Eds.), *Young Exceptional Children Monograph Series No. 3, Teaching strategies: What to do to support young children's development* (pp. 1-12). Longmont, CO: Sopris West.

McWilliam, R. (2005). DEC recommended practices: Interdisciplinary models. In S. Sandall, M. L. Hemmeter, B. J. Smith, & M. E. McLean (Eds.), *DEC recommended practices. A comprehensive guide for practical application in early intervention/early childhood special education* (pp. 127-146). Longmont, CO: Sopris West.

Sandall, S., Hemmeter, M. L., Smith, B. J., & McLean, M. E. (2005). *DEC recommended practices: A comprehensive guide for practical application in early intervention/early childhood special education.* Longmont, CO: Sopris West.

Stegelin, D. A. (2005). Making the case for play policy. Research-based reasons to support play-based environments. *Young Children, 60*(2), 76-85.

Ward, C. D. (1996). Adult intervention: Appropriate strategies for enriching the quality of children's play. *Young Children, 51*(3), 20-25.

Wilford, S. (2005, November). Sharing the power of play with parents. *Scholastic Early Childhood Today,* 18-19.

Social Mastery Motivation: Scaffolding Opportunities for Young Children

Patricia M. Blasco, Ph.D.
Oregon Health and Science University

*I*t is swim day for the Wee Care Child Center. Parents and young children, including children with disabilities, meet at the local YMCA once a month for a morning session arranged by the early intervention team. The locker room is always busy after the swim with toddlers, parents, and staff getting ready to go back to the center or home. Sarah's mom is helping her dry off and put on her clothes when there is a terrible scream. It frightens Sarah, and her mother turns to see that Jason, a child with autism, has fallen off the cement seat while his mother is preoccupied. Jane, the teacher, is also busy helping other children. Jason's mother quickly picks him up and holds him closely while the teacher tries to check his head and upper body for any injuries. He looks okay, but he continues to cry loudly with a high-pitched scream. Many of the children look upset and worried. After a few minutes, Jason starts to calm down and rocks in his mother's arms. Sarah's mother noticed Sarah's facial expression. She sees Sarah's worried look now has softened and expresses empathy. She asks Sarah if she would like to tell Jason that she is sorry he fell and offer him some Goldfish treats. Sarah shakes her head for yes, and her mother hands her the bag of Goldfish. Sarah hesitates, at first, and looks back at her mother who smiles encouragingly. Sarah says, "Sorry, Jason," and holds out the Goldfish. Jason doesn't acknowledge Sarah until his mother says, "Jason, Sarah has Goldfish for you." Jason looks at the bag and reaches in and takes some Goldfish. His mother says, "Jason, say thank you," which he does and continues to eat his Goldfish while being held by his mother. Sarah goes back to her mother and receives a big hug. "Good for you; you helped Jason feel better," says her mother.

The development of social skills and the ability to understand the appropriateness of social behavior across environments continues to be an issue for young children with disabilities as well as children who are considered at-risk for poor developmental outcomes. Changes in the Individuals With Disabilities Education Act (IDEA) have offered states

■▬▬▬▬▬▬▬▬▬▬▬▬■
There is a need to interpret and scaffold children's learning experiences in the area of social-emotional development.

the option of including children at risk for abuse and neglect among those who can be served under Part C. Infants and toddlers learn social skills from adults in their early environments and practice these skills in imitation and later in play with siblings and peers. For children at risk due to environmental or biological factors and children with disabilities, these behaviors often are not easily learned and generalized to social environments. Clearly, there is a need to interpret and scaffold children's learning experiences in the area of social-emotional development. Sarah's and Jason's mothers both helped their children engage in a social interaction. The steps leading to the interaction included practice of social goals that were supported by the parents. When children engage in goal-directed social learning, they are exhibiting social mastery motivation.

Understanding the Construct of Social Mastery Motivation

Social mastery motivation is defined as persistence in appropriate social interaction with adults and/or peers by initiating contact and/ or appropriate responses to others (Blasco, 1995; Hupp, Boat, Utke, & Connors, 1995; Hupp & Utke, 2001; MacTurk, Hunter, McCarthy, Vietze, & McQuiston, 1985). For example, in the previous vignette, two parents encouraged and supported their toddlers' initiations. *Social mastery motivation* is rooted in the theoretical conceptualizations of the broader construct of mastery motivation. In their seminal research, White (1959) and Hunt (1965) viewed mastery motivation as the desire to be competent. Just as *mastery motivation* is defined as persistence in cognitive tasks, *social mastery motivation* is defined as persistence in social tasks. The motivation to control and be effective in both problem-solving and social environments is thought to be intrinsically as well as extrinsically driven.

Social mastery motivation differs from social competence in that it is the driving motivation to impact the social environment that occurs prior to achieving social competence. The young child engaging in social mastery motivation is demonstrating emerging social abilities that are not yet mastered. *Social competence* is the ability to recognize, interpret, and respond appropriately in social situations (Kostelnik, Whiren, Soderman, Gregory, & Stein, 2002) so that the child has successful social interactions with adults and peers (Landry, 2006). The child's persistence in attempting social interactions to reach those social goals (Hupp & Utke, 2001) defines the construct of social mastery motivation.

Social Mastery Motivation and Children With Disabilities

Children with disabilities may have difficulty engaging in social interactions, as a result of either innate or environmental influences (Brown, Odom, & Conroy, 2001; Hauser-Cram, 1996, 1998). For example, a child with a seizure disorder may have difficulty interacting with his or her social environment due to the sedative effect of high levels of medication necessary to control the seizures (Hauser-Cram, 1996). In addition, researchers found that children with disabilities engaged primarily in solitary (Pierce-Jordan & Lifter, 2005) and parallel play (Bailey, McWilliam, Ware, & Burchinal, 1993) and rarely made social initiations to their typically developing peers (Blasco, Bailey, & Burchinal, 1993). Studies of children with disabilities have shown that young children need more than proximity to other young children in order to engage in appropriate social interactions (Odom, McConnell, & Chandler, 1993) and to increase peer-directed social communication (Craig-Unkefer & Kaiser, 2003). They need the encouragement and support of adults to guide their efforts at social initiations and social responsiveness.

When children engage in goal-directed social learning, they are exhibiting social mastery motivation.

Role of Caregivers and Scaffolding Social Mastery Motivation

As stated by Berk and Winsler (1995), "The social environment is the necessary scaffold, or support system, that allows the child to move forward and continue to build new competencies" (p. 26). It is imperative that caregivers (i.e., parents, service providers) help scaffold the child's early attempts at social mastery motivation. An important ingredient of this, then, is the caregiver's ability to understand and interpret social overtures made by the child and the child's ability to make those overtures first to adult caregivers and subsequently to peers. Keilty and Freund (2004) described an example of a specific social goal: a toddler asking for assistance with a spoon. The toddler's learning to request help is indicative of his or her social mastery motivation. Figure 1 demonstrates how the child's characteristics, including temperament and behavior, and parent/caregiver characteristics, including the ability to read cues and scaffold the child's social initiations and responses, lead to social mastery motivation and ultimately social competence. When a parent or caregiver reads the child's cue and responds appropriately, there is a "goodness of fit" between the child's characteristics and the parent's characteristics

Figure 1

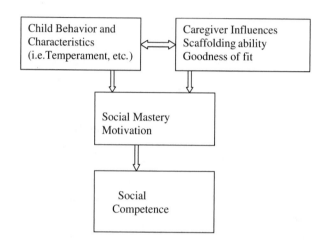

Scaffolding Social Mastery Motivation

✓ Hold and handle the child gently, watch his or her eyes for interest and change positions to improve access to toys and/or you
✓ Follow the child's initiations and expand on them
✓ Imitate the child's sounds and expressions
✓ Talk about the child's actions and your own actions
✓ Notice and respond to the child's interests and signals
✓ Help the child feel safe and secure to explore
✓ Emotionally support the child in mastering each step
✓ Demonstrate or model a new social skill
✓ Praise the child with specific feedback ("Good for you, you helped put toys away")
✓ Highlight the child's sense of mastery pleasure ("Doesn't that feel good?")
✓ Use firm words and actions to set limits and be consistent
✓ Offer appropriate choices so the child develops self-determination
✓ Observe, wait, and listen

Adapted from: P. M. Butterfield, C. A. Martin, & A. P. Prairie (2004). *Emotional connections: How relationships guide early learning*. Washington, DC: Zero to three.

(Thomas & Chess, 1977). Responsive interactions when the child has a disability may require the parent or caregiver to position oneself for face-to-face interactions, follow the child's lead and identify materials or objects that are of interest to the child (joint attention) and appropriate for his or her developmental level.

The following vignettes present ways in which parents and providers can scaffold social mastery motivation in infants and toddlers as well as prepare them for later social engagement with peers.

Juan, a 2-year-old who is in early intervention for speech and language concerns, is playing with his toys while his mother, Anita, and the early interventionist, Gail, are sitting with him. They are discussing ways to increase Juan's use of words in naturally occurring routines as he plays. Suddenly, Juan gets up and walks over to his mother and pushes her down on the floor, falling on top of her. Gail is puzzled by this reaction but Anita laughs. Anita tells Gail, this is one of their favorite games: "He pushes me down and then I hug him." Gail thinks about this as a natural opportunity to develop both language and social skills for Juan. She suggests to Anita that the next time Juan tries to push her over, to stay upright and ask, "What do you want?" After a pause, if Juan doesn't respond verbally, tell him "Say 'down please.'" This would help Juan develop his language skills as well as learn to ask for a social interaction with his mother.

Juan's mother is scaffolding social mastery by teaching Juan that a verbal request often precedes a social interaction. When he makes the request, he is rewarded by engaging in his favorite game and in getting a hug from his mother. In addition, the early interventionist used observation and clinical judgment to promote a learning opportunity during routines in the natural environment (Dunst, Bruder, Trivette, Raab, & McLean, 2001). When a provider combines what he or she knows to be recommended practices from research along with best clinical judgment, he or she is engaging in evidenced-based practice (Buysse & Wesley, 2006).

Children with disabilities may have difficulty engaging in social interactions as a result of either innate or environmental influences.

Table 1 presents social and emotional behaviors for infants who are typically developing. Infants with disabilities, however, may not exhibit typical milestones in social-emotional behavior at the same rate as typically developing children. Therefore, it is important that the parent and provider work together to document the individual child's abilities and

Table 1
Social and Emotional Behavior (Infants)

Age group	Behavior	Characteristics of behavior
1–3 months	Awareness of adult's voice	Differentiates familiar, loud, angry
	Cuddles	Calms when held or swaddled
	Maintains or avoids interaction	Coos at adult, smiles at adult, turns away from adult
4–8 months	Intentional communication	Reaches for, verbalizes
	Seeks attention	Vocalizes and/or seeks physical proximity
	Explores environment	Watches people and surrounding activities
	Shows preference for primary caregiver	Stays in physical contact while exploring
	Social games	Laughs, responds to pat-a-cake, peek-a-boo
8–12 months	Stranger anxiety	Clings to primary caregiver
	Independence	Resists caregiver's request
	Developing sense of self	Points and vocalizes to get desired object or person, offers toy or object

Note. From K. E. Allen & L. R. Marotz. (2003). *Developmental profiles: Pre-birth through twelve* (4th ed.) Albany, NY: Delmar; P. M. Blasco. (1995). Understanding the emotional and behavioral development of young children: Birth to 3 years. In T. J. Zirpoli (Ed.), *Understanding and affecting the behavior of young children* (pp. 34-59). Englewood Cliffs, NJ: Prentice-Hall; J. W. Gowen & J. B. Nebrig. (2002). *Enhancing early emotional development: Guiding parents of young children*. Baltimore: Brookes.

emerging skills through multiple sources of assessment information, including norm-referenced and curriculum-based measures, observation, and parent report (Blasco, 2001). In this way, parents and providers can set realistic social goals for the infant or toddler.

For example, for very young children with disabilities, adults may need to interpret their interests, especially if the child cannot physically move and explore the environment.

Joey is a 32-month-old who loves to play, but he has limited mobility due to spastic cerebral palsy. His mother is adept at reading his cues by watching his eyes and facial expressions. Since he was a baby, his mother would follow his gaze and then talk about the object of Joey's interest. For example, if he was looking at the family cat, Peaches, she would talk about Peaches and bring her to Joey. Joey has gotten along pretty well so far using his eyes and facial expression as his own communication system. His intervention team has discussed the importance of an augmentative communication device, but until he starts preschool, his mother doesn't think it is an issue.

Now the home visitor has brought along two assistive devices to teach Joey to say simple words such as hello *and* goodbye *in preparation for his transition to a preschool in the fall. The devices are easily programmed by having someone say a word that is recorded and then activated by a single switch. Joey's older brother says the words* hello *and* goodbye *into the devices. Joey demonstrates social mastery motivation by learning to use the switches appropriately. He smiles and vocalizes when he hears the phrases. To test his skill, his mother and the early interventionist take Joey to a neighborhood coffee shop that has a play area for children. His mother places his wheelchair near the play area and they set up the small devices on his table. Joey presses the right switch and says, "Hello." The children look at their parents, who smile encouragingly and then reply, "Hello." One little girl goes over to Joey and places a toy on his table. She asks, "Do you want to play too?" Joey just shakes his head yes; his mother and the early interventionist quickly realize that Joey's vocabulary will need to expand. After a while, it is time to go home. Joey selects* goodbye. *When the children say goodbye, he looks at his mother with a huge smile.*

Joey is rewarded for learning to initiate contact with other children by this appropriate play interaction in his local neighborhood. It is also an opportunity for his mother and the other team members to informally assess Joey's additional need for a more sophisticated communication system when he enters preschool. This system would expand his ability to interact socially and use his expressive vocabulary.

Toddlers are learning different social and emotional behaviors than infants. As stated earlier in this article, toddlers with disabilities learn social and emotional behaviors at rates that may differ from those of young children who are developing typically. In Table 2, social and emotional behaviors for toddlers are presented. It is important to observe the present level of social and behavioral development before introducing new social tasks to the child.

The roots of peer interaction are now observable as the toddler starts to move from parallel play to complementary and reciprocal play. This behavior occurs sequentially after the toddler has developed the ability

Table 2
Social and Emotional Development (Toddlers)

Age group	Behavior	Characteristics of behavior
12 months	Takes pleasure in mastery	Shows sense of accomplishment by smiling or clapping hands
	Enjoys hearing stories	Listens to stories read or told by adults
	Responds to adult praise	Looks at adult, may verbalize
18 months	Expresses ownership, possession	"It's mine" becomes favorite phrase
	Parallel play	Plays near other children, may watch and imitate others
	Sense of self-importance	Asserts rights, refers to self by name, tantrums
24–30 months	Develops empathy	Shows caring for others who are upset or hurt
	Begins sharing	Will occasionally share a toy
	Follows simple rules	Cleans up toys when requested
	Associative play	Plays with two or three friends
36 months	Cooperative play	Plays with groups, begins some dramatic play
	Turn taking	May engage in turn taking at times
	Aggression	May hit or grab a toy

Note. From K. E. Allen & L. R. Marotz. (2003). *Developmental profiles: Pre-birth through twelve* (4th ed.) Albany, NY: Delmar; P. M. Blasco. (1995). Understanding the emotional and behavioral development of young children: Birth to 3 years. In T. J. Zirpoli (Ed.), *Understanding and affecting the behavior of young children* (pp. 34-59). Englewood Cliffs, NJ: Prentice-Hall; J. W. Gowen & J. B. Nebrig. (2002). *Enhancing early emotional development: Guiding parents of young children.* Baltimore: Brookes.

to engage in symbolic (pretend) play (Howes, 1988). Complementary play may include give-and-take activities and turn taking. The child's ability to sustain his or her own wants and needs in order to share with others begins to increase as the child reaches his or her second birthday. Although the toddler is now engaging in reciprocal play, that play is typically directed toward one or two children within a group or toward a familiar adult. Social mastery motivation is demonstrated when a child is able to achieve a higher level of social play by mastering give-and-take activities and turn taking.

Sam is a 36-month-old who attends a community-based preschool while his mother works at a local bakery. Sam has a diagnosis of autism spectrum disorder and has difficulty taking turns or waiting for his turn at the preschool. The interventionist consults with his preschool teacher on strategies to make Sam's day successful. One idea the team developed was to make a social storybook about taking turns. The teacher took pictures of Sam and other children in the preschool taking turns during circle time, on the playground with play equipment, and in the cars-and-trucks area (Sam's favorite). Sam's mother reads the book to Sam before bed and they practice turn taking while he brushes his teeth with his sister.

Strategies to Support Social Mastery Motivation

In the vignette, Sam learned to take turns using a social story. His parents also used a social story to teach Sam to initiate a greeting with other children in a neighborhood preschool. Social stories have been used to teach children with disabilities the skills of choice making and social problem-solving (Barry & Burlew, 2004). Social stories can be created by providers working with parents or by parents as a tool for scaffolding their children's social play ability (see http://www.thegraycenter.org).

Children with disabilities generally learn social play in the same ways as their typically developing peers but at different rates. There is a noticeable difference, however, in the ability of children with disabilities to persist in attempts to learn more sophisticated levels of play (Blasco, 2001). It is important for caregivers and service providers to realize that children with disabilities may need help in reaching more sophisticated levels of social interactive play. If a toddler or young child is in a center-based program, providers should observe that child as well as other children to determine the level of play most frequently identified in the setting. If all children are engaging in lower or cursory levels of play such as solitary play, provide opportunities for sharing during routines such as circle time or snack. To encourage parallel play, have multiple sets of toys in play areas. For example, placing two sifters in the sandbox or two cars in the parking garage may encourage play. Arranging the room to encourage opportunities for play among two to three children at a time is another strategy used by providers. Some providers label the room by high-density areas and low-density areas and facilitate children's play in these areas as appropriate.

It is important for caregivers and service providers to realize that children with disabilities may need help in reaching more sophisticated levels of social interactive play.

To encourage more sophisticated play, adults can model behaviors and use peer models. A note of caution from one recent study: Children with pervasive developmental disorder were found to engage in social interaction less often during challenging play tasks (Pierce-Jordan & Lifter, 2005). Therefore, providers should start with activities that they know have been mastered by the child with a disability to encourage learning new social tasks.

Brown, Odom, and Conroy (2001) advocated for an intervention hierarchy for promoting peer social interactions. For example, a child with autism may need intensive strategies during which a teacher or assistant acts as a "buddy coach" to ensure the child stays with a peer, plays, and talks to the peer. The hierarchy is implemented in the same way as a response to intervention hierarchy, where the provider starts with the less-intensive strategies and employs more-intensive strategies when appropriate for the individual needs of the child. In this way the young child is more likely to be successful in social mastery motivation attempts.

Summary

Social mastery motivation has been recognized as an important construct in the early childhood and mental health fields. This construct is a precursor to social competence, because the child can persist at social tasks and caregivers can scaffold social experiences to make sure the child learns those skills and achieves social competence. Efforts to teach social skills to children using prompts such as storybooks or social stories are not new (Stanton-Chapman, Kaiser, & Wolery, 2006); however, research examining the application of these techniques with children under the age of 3 is still lagging. Those efforts need to be continued and evaluated for children under the age of 3.

Scaffolding by caregivers allows the child to develop social skills at a young age. It also provides the young child with opportunities to practice those skills with a nurturing caregiver. In addition, scaffolding helps children reorganize and regulate their behavior and avoid challenging or negative behaviors (Butterfield, Martin, & Prairie, 2004). Responsive caregivers anticipate challenging behaviors and help children find appropriate social solutions. It is also important to consider cultural perspectives when encouraging scaffolding strategies. Not every culture values independence or choice making; therefore, working closely with parents when setting social goals is important (Barrera, Corso, & MacPherson, 2003). By providing scaffolding for social and emotional behaviors, caregivers can set the stage for social mastery motivation and ultimately social competence for life.

Note

You may contact Patricia M. Blasco by e-mail at blascop@ohsu.edu

References

Bailey, D. B., McWilliam, R. A., Ware, W. B., & Burchinal, M. A. (1993). The social interactions of toddlers and preschoolers in same-age and mixed-age play groups. *Journal of Applied Developmental Psychology, 14,* 261-276.

Barrera, I., Corso, R. M., & MacPherson, D. (2003). *Skilled dialogue: Strategies for responding to cultural diversity in early childhood.* Baltimore: Brookes.

Barry, L. M., & Burlew, S. B. (2004). Using social stories to teach choice and play skills to children with autism. *Focus on Autism & Other Developmental Disabilities, 19*(1), 45-51.

Berk, L. E. & Winsler, A. (1995). *Scaffolding children's learning: Vygotsky and early childhood education.* Washington, DC: National Association of Education for Young Children.

Blasco, P. M. (2001). *Early intervention services for infant, toddlers, and their families.* Austin, TX: Pro-Ed.

Blasco, P. M., Bailey, D. B., & Burchinal, M. A. (1993). Dimensions of mastery in same-age and mixed-age integrated classrooms. *Early Childhood Research Quarterly, 8,* 193-206.

Blasco, P. M., Hrncir, E. J., & Blasco, P. (1990). The contributions of maternal involvement to mastery performance of infants with cerebral palsy. *Journal of Early Intervention, 14,* 161-174.

Boat, M. (1995). *Defining social mastery motivation in young children with or without disabilities.* Unpublished doctoral dissertation, University of Minnesota.

Brown, W. H., Odom, S. L., & Conroy, M. A. (2001). An intervention hierarchy for promoting young children's peer interactions in natural environments. *Topics in Early Childhood Special Education, 21,* 162-175.

Craig-Unkefer, L. A., & Kaiser, A. P. (2003). Increasing peer-directed social-communication skills of children enrolled in Head Start. *Journal of Early Intervention, 25,* 229-247.

Hauser-Cram, P. (1996). Mastery motivation in toddlers with developmental disabilities. *Child Development, 67,* 236-248.

Hauser-Cram, P. (1998). Research in review. I think I can, I think I can: Understanding and encouraging mastery motivation in young children. *Young Children, 53*(4), 67-71.

Howes, C. (1988). Peer interactions of young children. *Monographs of the Society for Research in Child Development, 53*(1), Series No. 217.

Hupp, S. C. (2000). *About social mastery motivation: Implications for educational practice.* Presented at the International Special Education Congress 2000, University of Manchester, Manchester, England.

Hupp, S. C., Boat, M. B., & Alpert, A. S. (1992). Impact of adult interaction on play behaviors and emotional responses of preschoolers with developmental delays. *Education and Training in Mental Retardation, 27,* 145-152.

Hupp, S. C., Boat, M. B., Utke, R. J., & Conyers, S. (1995). *Observation of social mastery, revised.* Unpublished manuscript, University of Minnesota, Department of Educational Psychology.

Keilty, B. & Freund, M. (2004). Mastery motivation: A framework for considering the "how" of infant and toddler learning. *Young Exceptional Children, 8*(1), 2-10.

Kostelnik, M., Whiren, A., Soderman, A. K., Gregory, K., & Stein, L. C. (2002). *Guiding children's social development: Theory to practice* (4th ed.). Albany, NY: Delmar.

Landry, S. (2006). *Pathways to competence: Encouraging healthy social and emotional development in young children*. Baltimore: Brookes.

MacTurk, R. H., Hunter, F. T., McCarthy, M. E., Vietze, P. M., & McQuiston, S. (1985). Social mastery motivation in Down syndrome and non-delayed infants. *Topics in Early Childhood and Special Education, 4,* 93-109.

Odom, S. L., McConnell, S. R., & Chandler, L. K. (1993). Acceptability and feasibility of classroom-based social interaction interventions for young children with disabilities. *Exceptional Children, 60,* 226-236.

Pierce-Jordan, S. & Lifter, K. (2005). Interaction of social and play behaviors in preschoolers with and without pervasive developmental disorder. *Topics in Early Childhood Special Education, 25,* 34-47.

Stanton-Chapman, T. L., Kaiser, A. P., & Wolery, M. (2006). Building social communication skills in Head Start children using storybooks: The effects of prompting on social interactions. *Journal of Early Intervention, 28,* 197-212.

White, R. W. (1959). Motivation reconsidered: The concept of competence. *Psychological Review, 66,* 297-333.

Increasing Communication and Language-Learning Opportunities for Infants and Toddlers

Dale Walker, Ph.D.,

Kathryn M. Bigelow, Ph.D.,
University of Kansas

Sanna Harjusola-Webb, Ph.D.,
Kent State University

The importance of communication and language development to the social and cognitive functioning of infants and toddlers is made clear when those abilities do not develop as expected (Warren & Walker, 2005). Communication and language deficits originating during early childhood can have a domino effect throughout a child's development, contributing in some instances to later learning disabilities or behavior disorders, as well as early reading and achievement deficits (e.g., Aram & Hall, 1989; Fey, Catts, & Larrivee, 1995; Scarborough, Dobrich, & Hager, 1991; Whitehurst & Lonigan, 1998). Because children who have delays in communication may be less likely to use communication skills during social situations, they may be more likely to use aggression or problem behavior to communicate (Hancock & Kaiser, 2006) and may eventually experience social isolation. When there are fewer opportunities for infants and toddlers to hear diverse, complex vocabulary or for them to have social exchanges where language is modeled and practiced, they are more likely to have smaller vocabularies at age 3 (Hart & Risley, 1995, 1999) and poorer literacy and readiness outcomes when they enter school compared with young children who have more positive early language-learning experiences (e.g., Burchinal et al., 2000; Dodici, Draper, & Peterson, 2003; Snow, Tabors, & Dickinson, 2001; Walker, Greenwood, Hart, & Carta, 1994). Therefore, delays in communication and language may significantly impact how young children access and participate in activities related to both social development and early literacy (Greenwood, Walker, & Utley, 2002; National Institute of Child Health and Human Development Child Care Research Network, 2000).

Tammy, an early childhood special education teacher and curriculum planner at an inclusive infant-toddler program that had both a home- and center-based component, understood how important communication and language development are for the infants and toddlers in her program. She noticed that those children who could initiate communication by pointing, signing, or using words were also much more likely to communicate with others and get positive attention from adults or peers. They were less likely to be frustrated, because they were able to communicate their wants and needs. Tammy wanted to strengthen the communication and language-learning opportunities provided to children in her classroom program. She decided to look for techniques that she could share with both program staff and parents to maximize children's opportunities across settings and routines. Tammy began looking for techniques that were found to be effective but at the same time easy to learn and implement with infants and toddlers who were at different developmental levels.

Intervention Approaches to Promote Communication

There are a number of evidence-based, naturalistic intervention approaches found to promote language and early literacy skills of infants and young children with and without disabilities. These intervention approaches have been developed to address communication and language intervention needs of children spanning diverse ages and developmental levels as well as intervention agents. Both milieu teaching and prelinguistic milieu teaching expand upon incidental teaching procedures introduced by Hart (1985) and are characterized by following a child's attentional lead, building social play routines, using prompts such as modeling, asking a question, or using time delay along with natural consequences such as giving the child the requested item when the child uses communication (e.g., Kaiser, Hancock, & Nietfeld, 2000; Warren, Yoder, Gazdag, Kim, & Jones, 1993; Yoder & Warren, 2002). Responsive interaction encourages adult responsiveness to child communication attempts and adult use of descriptive talk to increase a child's social communication (e.g., Kaiser & Delaney, 2001; Tannock & Girolametto, 1992; Trent-Stainbrook, Kaiser, & Frey, 2007). When using responsive interaction with young children, adults follow the child's attentional lead or interest and respond to the child's behavior

Communication and language deficits originating during early childhood can have a domino effect throughout a child's development.

using modeling, recasting, and expanding on the child's communication attempts without being directive or using prompts such as questions or requests for communication.

There have been successful demonstrations of these approaches for increasing the communication and language of infants, toddlers, and young children with parents (Alpert & Kaiser, 1992; Bigelow, 2006; Peterson, Carta, & Greenwood, 2005) and with teachers (e.g., Goldstein & Kaczmarek, 1992; Harjusola-Webb, 2006). These approaches have been used during activities such as book reading (Cole, Maddox, & Lim, 2006; Lonigan & Whitehurst, 1998) and when providing support for social interaction (e.g., Craig-Unkefer & Kaiser, 2002; Sandall, Schwartz, & Joseph, 2001). These intervention approaches also have been described in early childhood curricula and intervention guides (e.g., Notari-Syverson, O'Connor, & Vadasy, 2007; Pretti-Frontczak & Bricker, 2004; Sandall & Schwartz, 2002) and are included in the *Division for Early Childhood Recommended Practices* (Sandall, Hemmeter, Smith, & McLean, 2005).

Although there is ample evidence supporting the use of these practices and their benefits for infants and young children, they still are not frequently used in inclusive, community-based early childhood education and home-based programs (Gomez, Walls, & Baird, 2007; Roberts, Bailey, & Nychka, 1991; Schwartz, Carta, & Grant, 1996; Smith, Warren, Yoder, & Feurer, 2004; Walker, Harjusola-Webb, Small, Bigelow, & Kirk, 2005). A descriptive study of inclusive community-based child care programs revealed that, in general, early educators infrequently used language-promoting strategies such as following a child's lead, commenting, and shared book reading. When they did use these strategies, however, infants and toddlers were more likely to communicate using gestures and words (Walker et al., 2001). More recently, when we compared community-based early childhood programs that were assigned randomly to participate in either a project designed to provide them training on intervention strategies to promote communication or a contrast group in which providers would follow their regular practices, differences were found in communication levels for those infants and toddlers who were exposed more often to language-promoting strategies compared with children who did not receive the intervention in their early childhood classrooms (e.g., Walker, Bigelow, Powell, & Mark, 2007; Walker, Harjusola-Webb, & Atwater, 2008). In all cases, when naturalistic teaching strategies were used to promote communication, children showed gains in language-related outcomes.

It is important that infants and toddlers are provided with positive language-learning opportunities throughout their everyday experiences.

Given the association between early language, literacy, and personal/social competency and the development of successful relationships, school-readiness, and life-related skills, it is important that infants and toddlers are provided with positive language-learning opportunities throughout their everyday experiences. Furthermore, it is imperative that early childhood educators understand and use these evidence-based intervention strategies to improve the quality of the early language-learning experiences they provide for young children at risk for and with disabilities. This article describes eight functional, evidence-based strategies that may be used by early childhood educators, interventionists, and parents to provide infants and toddlers with language-learning opportunities across their daily routines and activities.

Table 1
Strategies for Promoting Communication

Strategy	Description
Arrange the environment	Organize a child's surroundings, materials, and schedule of routines to promote communication
Follow child's lead	Notice what a child is interested in, looking at, playing with, or talking about, and then use that interest to provide opportunities for communication
Comment and label	Name or describe the actions in which a child is involved or the toys or materials with which a child is playing
Imitate and expand	Repeat a child's vocalization or words back to the child and expand by providing new, more complex information
Use open-ended questions	Ask questions that begin with who, what, where, how, and why to encourage a child to answer with more than just yes or no
Planned delay/Fill in the blank	During a predictable phrase, song, or saying, pause and allow a child to fill in the blank
Give positive attention	Listen and respond to attempts to vocalize and use gestures or words to encourage further communication
Provide choices	Provide two or more options from which a child can choose

Strategies to Promote Communication of Infants and Toddlers

The following strategies (Table 1), derived from prelinguistic milieu, milieu teaching, incidental, and responsive teaching approaches previously described, can be used in early childhood education center- and home-based programs. They can be implemented easily by early childhood educators, parents, or other caregivers and are uniquely suited for use with infants and toddlers with diverse communication and language-learning needs. The highlighted strategies are presented here in an abridged format from a manual developed in collaboration with early childhood research partners (Walker, Small, Bigelow, Kirk, & Harjusola-Webb, 2004).

These language-promoting strategies have been designed to be implemented easily across a number of routines and activities, such as play, meals, book reading, circle time, diapering, and outings. Their consistent use during daily routines is especially beneficial because they help to create predictability in these routines. When children know what to expect, they are more likely to behave in a way that is appropriate to the routine. The additional benefit to using these strategies during daily routines is that they become part of the routine. Of course, it is imperative that in using these strategies, educators, care providers, and parents should be responsive to children's communication attempts. Merely using these strategies without listening to and responding to children's communication may work against the goal of increasing child communication. As adults use these strategies they must be sure to take turns with the child and encourage reciprocal interactions. In addition, it is very important that adults respond to the child's initiations and follow the child's lead in interactions in order to promote further communication and interaction. Children are then provided with natural repeated opportunities throughout each day to experience and practice communication.

1. Arrange the Environment

The environment in which the child learns comprises the physical structure of the classroom or areas within the home, the social interactions that occur, and the schedule of the day. Arrangement of the physical environment can involve a number of different strategies. By having a well-organized classroom or home environment, children can easily locate preferred toys or materials. See-through bins help to organize materials and make activities accessible to children and may help them independently choose and communicate about preferred activities. Bins placed slightly out of reach but within view encourage a child to request materials from the bins. Pictures of children, their families, teachers, and recent events placed low on the wall may pique a child's interest and provide opportunities to talk about the pictures or related topics.

A quiet book-reading area can help promote book reading and book activities. Soft seating areas with multiple seats/cushions can facilitate group book-reading sessions, as well as prompt children to independently initiate book activities throughout the day. Books can be organized so they are easily accessible to multiple children, including infants. Learning how books "work" and having opportunities to interact with books, both independently and with caregivers, is an important precursor to early literacy activities. During shared book-reading activities, caregivers should not be concerned that children will not sit still or listen to the whole book. Follow children's leads, talk about pictured actions and characters, allow children to turn pages, and respond to their communication attempts.

Daily routines and transitions from one activity to another are another aspect of the environment. Posting and following a daily schedule can provide a general structure for the day and thus provide some predictability for children. For toddlers and older children, pictures may be used to depict daily activities so that children can anticipate and name upcoming activities. Talking about the day's schedule, in addition to providing an opportunity for communication, provides them with a reminder of what can be expected. Predictable routines for activities such as eating breakfast, cleaning up, diapering, or going outside also can include a clearly marked activity starter. One common example of this is use of a "cleanup" song. Furthermore, transitions between activities can be a challenging time for many children, so planning for transitions and avoiding children's waiting for others or directives can not only avoid problems but make these positive learning times. Finally, setting a regular time for book activities and story time, and, as much as possible, sticking to those times each day; providing additional opportunities for book activities throughout the day; and responding to children's initiations to look at books together or independently all help prepare the classroom or home environment with a supportive foundation for promoting communication. The remaining seven strategies can be used during interactions with infants and toddlers more easily once these environmental arrangements are in place.

2. Follow Child's Lead

This strategy involves two steps: noticing what a child is interested in, looking at, playing with, or talking about and then using that interest to provide opportunities for communication. Children are more likely to attend to activities or objects of their choosing. Following a child's lead increases the likelihood that he or she will be interested in communicating about an activity. Notice children's activities and current interests and then label, describe, and ask questions about that interest. Expand upon or imitate what a child says about that interest. Ask questions and respond to what children say. As children's interests change, continue following their lead to further their engagement in the new activity.

Sometimes children are not engaged in an activity. In this situation, present a couple choices based on activities in which the child has shown interest in the past. Then, follow the child's lead in that activity or as he or she moves on to new interests. Offering choices not only gives children more options but also provides the opportunity to communicate their interests.

Following a child's lead increases the likelihood that he or she will be interested in communicating about an activity.

Following a child's lead is important in that it is a foundation for the remaining six strategies. For other strategies to be effective, it is important to follow the child's lead to assure attention, engagement, and interest.

3. Comment and Label

This strategy involves naming or describing the actions in which a child is involved and the toys or materials with which a child is playing. Commenting and labeling can give children opportunities to hear how we talk about our surroundings and actions and teach correct labels for the actions or objects a child sees. When children hear more words, hear how they are used, and see how people communicate, they will be more likely to use gestures, vocalizations, and words to communicate their needs and wants. For example, care providers might name the child's toys, materials, or actions. For infants, one might say "Ball," whereas "You bounced that ball so high!" is more appropriate for toddlers. While changing diapers, you might name body parts, as well as describe what you are doing as you do it, for example: "I've got your feet; see your toes? I'm taking your diaper off, and here is your clean diaper." During book activities, talk about the pictures, name objects to which a child points, and describe characters' actions. Comment on the story as you read it, providing new information and responding to children's interests. Following children's leads while using these strategies ensures that children remain engaged and interested in the activity.

4. Imitate and Expand

Imitating is repeating a child's vocalizations or words back to the child, whereas *expanding* is repeating what a child has just said and adding new, more complex information. These strategies are important, because they show the child that he or she was heard and understood.

For example, if a child's words are unclear, imitating allows the child to know you heard them and possibly (if you inferred his/her intent) hear the correct form of pronunciation. Expanding can be an effective way to teach new information. With infants, imitate the child's vocalizations and often, infants will repeat that sound back to you again. Toddlers might use single words or approximations of words, such as "ba ba" for bottle. Repeat back the correct form of the word or expand on that vocalization by saying "Bottle, please." Expanding allows you to provide additional, more complex information that may introduce new words or concepts. A child might say "I clean" while wiping a table. An adult might say "Yes, you're cleaning the table with a towel."

5. Use Open-Ended Questions

This format for asking questions permits children to respond in multiple ways rather than simply answering yes or no or nodding their heads. These questions might begin with what, who, where, how, or why, providing opportunities for children to communicate and engage in explicit or lengthier conversations. As with the other strategies, it is important to follow children's leads. A child is more likely to respond to questions pertaining to the activity in which he or she is already involved than to questions unrelated to the child's current interests.

Ask questions related to what the child is playing or doing, what materials the child is using, or his or her daily routine. Questions that allow a child to direct play or activities may help to sustain that activity and promote communication. Asking questions such as "What should we build?" allows children to take the lead in your joint activities. While looking at familiar books, ask questions about the pictures, the characters, and their actions. Ask questions that allow for predictions as well, for example: "What do you think is going to happen next?" If a child does not or cannot answer your question, answer that question yourself and continue talking about the child's interests with comments and labels, imitating and expanding.

Questions that allow a child to direct play or activities may help to sustain that activity and promote communication.

6. Planned Delay/Fill in the Blank

This strategy refers to inserting a planned delay during a predictable routine that can promote a child's communication. This strategy is used during joint activities in which children know what to expect, and can "fill in the blank" in a song or common phrase. Pausing after singing "Twinkle, twinkle, little…" and allowing the child to fill in "star" is one example of fill in the blank. This allows children to show you what they know and can say, and it emphasizes success while minimizing the need for corrections. This strategy also may be used while looking at a familiar book together. If the child knows the story well enough to fill in key words, an adult can initiate a phrase from the book, leave out a key word, and wait 3 to 5 seconds. If the child does not respond, fill in the blank yourself and continue with the activity. Interactions should remain positive, so it is not crucial that the child provide a specific response.

7. Give Positive Attention

Providing positive attention involves attending and responding to infants and toddlers when they attempt to vocalize or use gestures or words. Listening and responding to children's talk as well as providing positive comments, praise, or your attention lets children know they have been heard and encourages them to continue to make additional communication attempts in the future. Positive comments about children's communication, such as "Thanks for telling me what you want," create more opportunities for practice. These opportunities to provide positive attention and praise occur throughout each day. Prohibitions such as saying "No" or "Don't do that" inhibit children from attempting to communicate and thus limit opportunities for practicing language. Getting down at eye level and attending to a child who is reading a book aloud or a group of children who are talking about their activity reinforces those attempts at communication and encourages future attempts as well.

8. Provide Choices

Providing two or more options from which to choose can prompt children to communicate their needs and desires. By providing choices, children are provided with an opportunity to practice communication and language by talking about things of preference and possibly familiarity in their environment. There are multiple opportunities throughout each day to provide a choice of toys, materials, or activities. Two examples are, "Would you like to play with the cars or the animals?" or, "Would you like to read on the floor or on a chair?" For younger children, simply holding up two toys, for example, a block and a doll, can prompt a child to point to or reach for what he or she wants, thereby engaging the child's interest and allowing you an opportunity to follow his or her lead. Being presented with two visual choices, in addition to being presented with the choice verbally, can help the child make that choice. Giving choices also can help to avoid challenging behavior. At cleanup time, ask "Would you like to pick up the cars or the blocks?" If children refuse to complete a task, ask "Would you like to do it yourself or would you like help?" In book activities, provide choices throughout the day by making a variety of books available to children. For example, allow children to choose the books that will be used during circle time, bedtime, or other routines and present two to three options instead of a whole bin or shelf full of books.

Planning to Use the Strategies

It is important to note that there is much flexibility in how each of these language-promoting strategies is used. It is not essential to use all of them in every interaction with every child. Caregivers may find that they use some strategies more than others, and this may depend on the activity or the child. The strategies are to be used flexibly to meet an individual child's needs. It is often through continued use that care providers learn how children respond to particular strategies. Some care providers just find themselves using some strategies more than others. *Follow child's lead, Comment and label*, and *Ask open-ended questions* are strategies likely to be used more frequently and in more varied situations than *Planned delay/Fill in the blank*. Thus, many care providers have found it helpful to learn all of the strategies so that they can use them all comfortably when appropriate. Some care providers have found it helpful to post a list of these strategies (see Table 1) in a place they can refer to frequently, and they use them across the numerous opportunities that arise throughout the day to promote communication.

There is much flexibility in how each of these language-promoting strategies is used.

After reading about the language-promoting strategies, Tammy thought about which strategies she was most comfortable implementing in her classroom and recommending for her program. She decided to start by focusing on just a few of the strategies. She also decided to make some changes in the layout of her classroom using the environmental arrangements strategies, but she decided to make those changes slowly as she began to use the other strategies. To begin, she used a planning form to describe current communication patterns and preferred activities for two children in her program—Marcus and Briana. She then thought about how she could best apply some of these strategies in their preferred activities and listed her ideas. She decided to post the strategies as a reminder of her plans. As she began implementing the strategies, she immediately noticed that the children's attempts to communicate were more frequent when she used the strategies. Furthermore, she felt that the strategies were easy to implement, and she quickly looked forward to trying out more of the strategies in other activities and with other children.

Supporting Implementation of the Strategies

It can be intimidating to try to begin using all of these strategies throughout each day. Many care providers report that it is helpful to choose two or three strategies described in the *Promoting Communication Manual* (Walker et al., 2004) to use during a few specific activities, such as mealtime or when playing with infants and toddlers, and then gradually add the remaining strategies as they become more comfortable and confident in their use. Table 2 provides an example of a form used to plan implementation of these strategies. This Promoting Communication Planning Form helps educators and parents identify current communication skills and preferred activities for each child with whom they are working. This information can then help the team determine the strategies it will begin using with each child, and the activities in which those strategies will be

Table 2
Sample Promoting Communication Plan for Tammy's Panda Room

Child	Communication at this time	Preferred activities	Strategies I can use
Marcus	- Some pointing	- Animals	- Follow his lead in animal play
	- A few single-word approximations	- Picture books	-Label animals, describe animal activities
			- Books available throughout day
			- Follow his lead and comment and label pictures in books
			- Respond to and imitate his single words
Briana	- Many single words	- Dress up	- Ask open-ended questions about dress-up activity
	- A few two-word combinations	- Dress up	- Expand on her words by offering more information about dress-up activity
		- Lunch/ snack	- Label food choices, cup, and plate
			- Provide choices of where to sit and foods to eat

used. It also can be revised over time to address changes in children's communication and to incorporate additional strategies as appropriate.

Another tool that might be used by early educators, parents, and other caregivers to monitor their use of the communication strategies is the Communication Promotion Checklist (Figure 1). This fidelity checklist (Walker, Bigelow, Harjusola-Webb, Small, & Kirk, 2004) allows early childhood care and education providers or program directors, as well as parents, to rate how often they use each strategy throughout daily routines and activities. On this form, each strategy is rated as having been used "often," "sometimes," "rarely," or "not today" during activities such as play, toileting, circle time, and outdoor time. There is no specified length of

Figure 1
Early Educator, Program Director, and Parent Communication Promotion Checklist

		Freeplay	Toileting/Care	Mealtimes	Outdoors	Outings	other:
Parent/Caregiver: _____ Date: _____ Observer if different: _____		Not Today / Rarely / Sometimes / Often	Not Today / Rarely / Sometimes / Often		Not Today / Rarely / Sometimes / Often		
Followed Children's Lead *Goal: 10-20 per 30 min.	Noticed and followed child's interest, play, and talk	N R S O	N R S O	N R S O	N R S O	N R S O	N R S O
Commented and Labeled *Goal: 20-30 per 30 min.	Described actions, toys, or activities	N R S O	N R S O	N R S O	N R S O	N R S O	N R S O
Imitated and Expanded *Goal: 5-15 per 30 min.	Imitated child talk and expanded by adding new info	N R S O	N R S O	N R S O	N R S O	N R S O	N R S O
Asked Questions *Goal: 15-25 per 30 min.	Asked open-ended questions, "What, who, why, how..."	N R S O	N R S O	N R S O	N R S O	N R S O	N R S O
Used Fill in the Blank/Delay *Goal: 1-5 per 30 min.	Allowed child to fill in the blank in a song/common phrase	N R S O	N R S O	N R S O	N R S O	N R S O	N R S O
Used positive feedback/praise/attention	Was positive about behavior and talk *Goal: 5-10 per 30 min.	N R S O	N R S O	N R S O	N R S O	N R S O	N R S O
Provided choices *Goal: 1-5 per 30 min.	Allowed child to choose from more than one activity	N R S O	N R S O	N R S O	N R S O	N R S O	N R S O

Environmental Arrangement Strategies

Books and book activities provided	yes no	Materials out, available and arranged	yes no
Books available throughout the day; areas to look at books	☐ ☐	Toys, materials out, arranged	☐ ☐
Comments:			

© 2004 University of Kansas, Promoting Communication Strategies Checklist: Home (Reproduce with Permission Only) Walkard@ku.edu

observation for those using this form; it is designed to be very flexible in its use. Some care providers rate their use of strategies across the entire day, whereas others break their day down into specific activities. Some record use of strategies for a specific length of time, whereas others simply record for the length of the given activity. As long as each care provider or parent is using the form in a consistent manner, the information collected using this form can provide valuable feedback about reported use of the strategies over time. General guidelines are provided on the form based on the average frequency of implementation of each strategy observed being used in programs involved in the intervention. When completed, the checklist gives an estimate of how frequently the language-promoting strategies were used. In addition, the checklist may be used as a guide to assist early care and education providers and parents in their effort to promote children's communication across activities and to maximize the opportunities for child communication growth and development.

Monitoring the communication progress of infants and young children also may be accomplished through the use of a progress-monitoring tool such as the Early Communication Indicator, which is an Individual Growth and Development Indicator (IGDI) (e.g., Carta et al., 2002; Kirk, 2006; Walker, Carta, Greenwood, & Buzhardt, 2008). Through this approach, semistructured, play-based progress-monitoring assessments are conducted and graphical displays of child progress may be used to guide intervention decision making and for progress monitoring. Further information about the IGDIs may be accessed on the Internet (http://www.igdi.ku.edu).

A systematic progress-monitoring approach is an important component of language intervention efforts targeting infants and toddlers, particularly those at risk for or with identified disabilities. When educators or other early childhood professionals monitor child progress in specific outcome areas, such as language, they increase their capacity to identify children in need of additional or different forms of intervention, and changes in instructional or intervention efforts may be made accordingly.

Using Strategies to Promote Communication in Your Program

The communication-promoting intervention strategies reviewed here are ones that may be incorporated easily into ongoing routines and activities in early childhood education programs and in homes and may be used in conjunction with other early childhood curricula and interventions, as well as with progress-monitoring tools. Using these naturalistic strategies increases the language-learning opportunities presented to infants and toddlers, and in doing so, helps to promote early communication and literacy development.

Tammy chose to use multiple means to monitor the children's language development as well as the teaching staff's actual implementation of the communication strategies. The information gathered from self-checks, progress monitoring, and child outcome measures provided useful information for Tammy when discussing her language curriculum with the center staff and parents. The center director, teachers, and parents were excited to see documentation of the children's progress, and Tammy was able to make suggestions for home visitors and parents regarding how to use the communication strategies at home as well. This new system of ongoing measurement of intervention fidelity and progress monitoring gave Tammy confidence that the strategies were being used consistently and verified that the children in her early childhood program were making measurable gains on their communication goals.

Notes

Dale Walker may be contacted by email at walkerd@ku.edu

Preparation of this manuscript was supported by Grants H324C020078 and H326M070005 funded by the Office of Special Education Programs, U.S. Department of Education Grants and by the Kansas Intellectual and Developmental Disabilities Research Center, NIH HD002528. The opinions expressed herein do not necessarily reflect the position or policy of the U.S. Office of Education and no official endorsement by the U.S. Office of Education should be inferred.

The authors would like to thank all past and present team members of the Promoting Communication for Infants and Toddlers Project for their participation in this work, especially Drs. Cathy Small, Stacie Kirk, and Carla Peterson, as well as John Powell and Natalie Mark. Deepest gratitude is extended to Dr. Betty Hart for her continued support and inspiration for this work.

References

Alpert, C. L. & Kaiser, A. P. (1992). Training parents as milieu language teachers. *Journal of Early Intervention, 16*, 31-52.

Aram, D. M. & Hall, N. E. (1989). Longitudinal follow-up of children with preschool communication disorders: Treatment implications. *School Psychology Review, 18,* 487-501.

Bigelow, K. M. (2006). *Communication promotion and planned activities with families experiencing multiple risks.* Doctoral dissertation, University of Kansas. Retrieved April 10, 2008, from ProQuest Digital Dissertations database. (Publication No. AAT 3214822)

Burchinal, M. R., Roberts, J. E., Riggins, R., Jr., Zeisel, S. A., Neebe, E., & Bryant, D. (2000). Relating quality of center-based child care to early cognitive and language development longitudinally. *Child Development, 71,* 339-357.

Carta, J. J., Greenwood, C. R., Walker, D., Kaminski, R., Good, R., McConnell, S., McEvoy, M. (2002). Individual growth and development indicators (IGDIs): Assessment that guides intervention for young children. In: M. Ostrosky & E. Horn (Eds.) *Young Exceptional Children Monograph Series, No. 4, Assessment: Gathering Meaningful Information* (pp. 5-28). Longmont, CO: Sopris West.

Cole, K., Maddox, M., & Lim, Y. S. (2006). Language is the key: Constructive interactions around books and play. In R. McCauley & M. E. Fey (Eds.), *Treatment of language disorders in children* (pp. 149-173). Baltimore: Brookes.

Craig-Unkefer, L. A. & Kaiser, A. P. (2002). Improving the social communication skills of at-risk preschool children in a play context. *Topics in Early Childhood Special Education, 22,* 3-13.

Dodici, B. J., Draper, D. C., & Peterson, C. A. (2003). Early parent-child interactions and early literacy development. *Topics in Early Childhood Special Education, 23,* 124-136.

Fey, M. E., Catts, H., & Larrivee, L. S. (1995). Preparing preschoolers for the academic and social challenges of school. In M. E. Fey, J. Windsor, & S. F. Warren (Eds.), *Language intervention in preschool through the elementary years* (pp. 225-290). Baltimore: Brookes.

Goldstein, H. & Kaczmarek, L. (1992). Promoting communicative interaction among children in integrated intervention settings. In S. F. Warren & J. Reichle (Eds.), *Causes and effects in communication and language intervention* (pp. 81-111). Baltimore: Brookes.

Gomez, C. R., Walls, S., & Baird, S. (2007). On the same page: Seeing fidelity of intervention. *Young Exceptional Children, 10*(4), 20-29.

Greenwood, C. R., Walker, D., & Utley, C. A. (2002). Social-communicative skills and life achievements. In H. Goldstein, L. Kaczmarek, & K. M. English (Eds.), *Promoting social competence in children and youth with developmental disabilities* (Vol. 10, pp. 345-370). Baltimore: Brookes.

Hancock, T. B. & Kaiser, A. P. (2006). Enhanced milieu teaching. In R. McCauley & M. E. Fey (Eds.), *Treatment of language disorders in children* (pp. 203-236). Baltimore: Brookes.

Harjusola-Webb, S. M. (2006). The use of naturalistic communication intervention with young children who have developmental disabilities. (Doctoral dissertation, University of Kansas, 2006). *Dissertation Abstracts International, A 67/04,* 1290. (Publication No. AAT 3216284)

Hart, B. (1985). Naturalistic language training techniques. In S. F. Warren & A. K. Rogers-Warren (Eds.), *Teaching functional language.* Baltimore: University Park Press.

Hart, B. & Risley, T. R. (1995). *Meaningful differences in the everyday experience of young American children.* Baltimore: Brookes.

Hart, B. & Risley, T. R. (1999). *The social world of children learning to talk.* Baltimore: Brookes.

Kaiser, A. P. & Delaney, E. M. (2001). Responsive conversations: Creating opportunities for naturalistic language teaching. In M. Ostrosky & S. Sandall (Eds.), *Young Exceptional Children Monograph Series, No. 3, Teaching strategies: What to do support young children's development* (pp. 13-23). Longmont, CO: Sopris West.

Kaiser, A. P., Hancock, T. B., & Nietfeld, J. P. (2000). The effects of parent-implemented enhanced milieu teaching on the social communication of children who have autism [Special issue]. *Journal of Early Education and Development, 4,* 423-446.

Kirk, S. (2006). The effects of using outcome measures and progress monitoring to guide language-promoting interventions in Early Head Start Programs. (Doctoral Dissertation, University of Kansas, Lawrence, KS). *Dissertation Abstracts International, A 67/02,* 519. (Publication No. AAT 3207867)

Lonigan, C. J. & Whitehurst, G. J. (1998). Relative efficacy of parent and teacher involvement in a shared-reading intervention for preschool children from low-income backgrounds. *Early Childhood Research Quarterly, 13,* 263-290.

National Institute for Child Health and Human Development Early Child Care Research Network. (2000). The relation of child care to cognitive and language development. *Child Development, 71,* 960-980.

Notari-Syverson, A., O'Connor, R., & Vadasy, P. F. (2007). *Ladders to literacy: A preschool activity book* (2nd ed.). Baltimore: Brookes.

Peterson, P., Carta, J. J., & Greenwood, C. R. (2005). Teaching enhanced milieu language teaching skills to parents in multiple risk families. *Journal of Early Intervention, 27,* 94-109.

Roberts, J. E., Bailey, D. B., & Nychka, H. B. (1991). Teachers' use of strategies to facilitate the communication of preschool children with disabilities. *Journal of Early Intervention, 15,* 358-376.

Pretti-Frontczak, K. & Bricker, D. (2004). *An activity-based approach to early intervention* (3rd ed.). Baltimore: Brookes.

Sandall, S., Hemmeter, M. L., Smith, B. J., & McLean, M. E. (Eds.) (2005). *DEC recommended practices: A comprehensive guide for practical application in early intervention/early childhood special education.* Longmont, CO: Sopris West.

Sandall, S. & Schwartz, I. S. (2002). *Building blocks for teaching preschoolers with special needs.* Baltimore: Brookes.

Sandall, S., Schwartz, I., & Joseph, G. (2001). A building blocks model for effective instruction in inclusive early childhood settings. *Young Exceptional Children, 4*(3), 3-9.

Scarborough, H. S., Dobrich, W., & Hager, M. (1991). Preschool literacy experience and later reading achievement. *Journal of Learning Disabilities, 24,* 508-511.

Schwartz, I., Carta, J. J., & Grant, S. (1996). Examining the use of recommended language-intervention practices in early childhood special education classrooms. *Topics Early Childhood Special Education, 16,* 251-272.

Smith, J. D., Warren, S. F., Yoder, P. J., & Feurer, I. (2004). Teachers' use of naturalistic communication intervention practices. *Journal of Early Intervention, 27,* (1-14).

Snow, C. E., Tabors, P. O., & Dickinson, D. K. (2001). Language development in the preschool years. In D. K. Dickinson & P. O. Tabors (Eds.), *Beginning literacy with language* (pp. 1-23). Baltimore: Brookes.

Tannock, R. & Girolametto, L. (1992). Reassessing parent-focused language intervention programs. In S. F. Warren & J. Reichle (Eds.), *Causes and effects in communication and language intervention* (pp. 49-76). Baltimore: Brookes.

Trent-Stainbrook, A., Kaiser, A. P., & Frey, J. R. (2007). Older siblings' use of responsive interaction strategies and effects on their younger siblings with Down syndrome. *Journal of Early Intervention, 29,* 273-286.

Walker, D., Bigelow, K., Harjusola-Webb, S., Small, C., & Kirk, S. (2004). *Promoting communication strategies checklists: Fidelity, program and home.* Lawrence: University of Kansas, Schiefelbusch Institute for Life Span Studies, Juniper Gardens Children's Project.

Walker, D., Bigelow, K., Powell, J., & Mark, N. C. (2007, October). *Fidelity and dosage of communication strategies used by child care educators.* Symposium presented at the Division for Early Childhood International Conference, Niagara Falls, Ontario, Canada.

Walker, D., Carta, J. J., Greenwood, C. R., & Buzhardt, J. F. (2008). The use of individual growth and developmental indicators for progress monitoring and intervention decision making in early education. *Exceptionality, 16,* 33-47.

Walker, D., Greenwood, C. R., Hart, B., & Carta, J. J. (1994). Improving the prediction of early school academic outcomes using socioeconomic status and early language production. *Child Development, 65,* 606-621.

Walker, D., Harjusola-Webb, S., & Atwater, J. B. (2008, February). *Using measurement of intervention fidelity and child communication outcomes to increase early educator's use of strategies to promote communication of infants and toddlers.* Poster presented at the Conference for Research Innovation in Early Intervention, San Diego, CA.

Walker, D., Harjusola-Webb, S., Small, C., Bigelow, K., & Kirk, S. M. (2005). Forming research partnerships to promote communication of infants and young children in child care. In: E. Horn, M. Ostrosky, & H. Jones (Eds.). *Young Exceptional Children Monograph,* Series No. 6, Interdisciplinary Teams, 69-81.

Walker, D., Linebarger, D. L., Bigelow, K. M., Harjusola-Webb, S., Small, C. J., Rodrigues, D., et al. (2001, April). *Language interactions related to quality of infant childcare.* Poster presented at the Biennial Meeting for the Society for Research in Child Development, Minneapolis, MN.

Walker, D., Small, C., Bigelow, K., Kirk, S., & Harjusola-Webb, S. (2004). *Strategies for promoting communication and language of infants and toddlers manual.* Lawrence: University of Kansas, Schiefelbusch Institute for Life Span Studies, Juniper Gardens Children's Project.

Warren, S. F. & Walker, D. (2005). Fostering early communication and language development. In D. M. Teti (Ed.), *Handbook of research methods in developmental science* (pp. 249-270). Malden, MA: Blackwell Publishing.

Warren, S. F., Yoder, P., J., Gazdag, G. E., Kim, K., & Jones, H. A. (1993). Facilitating prelinguistic communication skills in young children with developmental delay. *Journal of Speech and Hearing Research, 36,* 83-97.

Whitehurst, G. J., & Lonigan, C. J. (1998). Child development and emergent literacy. *Child Development, 69,* 848-872.

Yoder, P. J. & Warren, S. F. (2002). Effects of prelinguistic milieu teaching and parent responsivity education on dyads involving children with intellectual disabilities. *Journal of Speech, Language, and Hearing Research, 44,* 224-237.

Resources
Within Reason

Measuring the Outcomes of Interventions for Infants, Toddlers, and Their Families

Anne Brager, M.S., R.N.
Frederick County Infants and Toddlers Program, Frederick, MD

Camille Catlett, M.A.
University of North Carolina at Chapel Hill

Accountability is an integral part of providing effective interventions for infants and toddlers and their families. Early childhood providers, programs, and agencies need to be able to document how their services and supports are making a difference for children and families. This section features resources that explain key concepts and practices related to measuring child and family outcomes.

Position Statements

Promoting Positive Outcomes for Children With Disabilities: Recommendations for Curriculum, Assessment, and Program Evaluation

This paper has been developed by the Division for Early Childhood (DEC) of the Council for Exceptional Children (CEC) to serve as a companion document to the 2003 joint position statement *Early Childhood Curriculum, Assessment and Program Evaluation: Building an Effective, Accountable System in Programs for Children Birth through Age 8* from National Association for the Education of Young Children (NAEYC) and National Association of Early Childhood Specialists in State Departments of Education (NAECS/SDE) (http://www.naeyc.org/about/positions/pdf/CAPEexpand.pdf).

http://www.dec-sped.org/pdf/positionpapers/Prmtg_Pos_Outcomes_Companion_Paper.pdf

Measures

Program Assessment Rating Tool (PART)

The Program Assessment Rating Tool, or PART for short, is a questionnaire designed to help assess the management and performance of programs. It is used to evaluate a program's purpose, design, planning, management, results, and accountability to determine its overall effectiveness. A related site shows performance ratings for all federal programs, including Part C and Preschool Special Education Section 619 of Part B.

http://www.whitehouse.gov/omb/expectmore/part.html (Questionnaire)

http://www.whitehouse.gov/omb/part/ (Performance ratings for federal programs)

Print Resources

Hebbeler, K., & Barton, L. (2007). The need for data on child and family outcomes at the federal and state levels. *Young Exceptional Children Monograph Series, 9,* 1–15.

This article describes events and issues related to the current federal requirements for reporting outcomes on children and families served through IDEA Part C and children served through Part B Preschool. Critical events leading up to the current requirements are summarized. This is followed by a discussion of options for the design and implementation of state outcome measurement systems and the implications of outcome measurement for children and families and the programs serving them.

Web Resources

Accountability in Early Childhood: No Easy Answers

In this Occasional Paper published by the Herr Research Center for Children and Social Policy of the Erikson Institute, Samuel J. Meisels discusses the practical concerns of high-stakes testing of young children.

http://72.32.138.202/downloads/cmsFile.ashx?VersionID=1785&PropertyID=78

Accountability Systems: Improving Results for Young Children

This brief presents key principles of effective accountability systems, describes basic steps to develop an accountability system for programs serving young children and discusses trade-offs inherent in designing such systems. It also shares examples of state and local systems.

http://www.financeproject.org/Publications/accountability.pdf

Assessment and Accountability for Programs Serving Young Children With Disabilities

Kathleen Hebbeler, Lauren R. Barton, and Sangeeta Mallik's article reviews issues related to the use of assessments in providing outcome data, discusses challenges in conducting valid assessments for accountability purposes, and outlines decisions states must make related to assessment as they design and implement outcome measurement approaches. The use of standardized or curriculum-based measures is discussed, along with other choices related to the use of assessment for accountability.

http://www.fpg.unc.edu/~eco/pdfs/Assessment_Accoutability_6-27-07_.pdf

Child and Family Outcomes

The National Early Childhood Technical Assistance Center (NECTAC) regularly updates this Web site, which describes requirements of, and provides resources, examples, and tools related to child and family outcomes.

http://www.nectac.org/topics/quality/childfam.asp

Early Childhood Outcomes (ECO) Center

The U.S. Department of Education–funded ECO Center supports the study, development, and implementation of child and family outcome measures for infants, toddlers, and preschoolers with disabilities. The ECO Center Web site features many downloadable resources and measures for use in accountability systems. For example, click on Activities & Outcomes, then again on Q & A to see a summary of answers to frequently asked questions.

http://www.fpg.unc.edu/~eco/

Implementing Results-Based Decision-Making: Advice From the Field

Written for the National Governors Association Center for Best Practices and The Finance Project, this report is based on interviews with more than 50 leaders in the field who provide advice on measuring the success of their supports for children and families by the results or outcomes they achieve. It covers various dimensions of results-based decision-making, including strategic planning that logically connects strategies to outcomes.

http://www.fpg.unc.edu/~eco/pdfs/1999WELFAREBARRIERS.pdf

Issues in Designing State Accountability Systems

This working document written by Gloria Harbin, Beth Rous, and Mary McLean is designed to support state policy makers and researchers who are interested in collaboratively designing and implementing rigorous and systematic accountability models that yield accurate data. Background information on federal reporting requirements is included.

http://www.ihdi.uky.edu/Sparc/Issues_in_Accountability.pdf

Join the Party: Engaging Stakeholders

This document written by Larry Edelman provides many useful tools, worksheets, and charts for engaging stakeholders and guiding teams through the change process.

http://www.fpg.unc.edu/~eco/pdfs/EdelmanJoinParty.pdf

Matrix of Research on Early Childhood Education Outcomes

The Public Policy Forum recently created a matrix of research on early childhood education comparing outcomes across studies. Overall, it shows that existing research supports the connection between higher quality early childhood programs and long-term benefits in a number of areas.

http://www.publicpolicyforum.org/Matrix.htm

National Center for Special Education Accountability Monitoring (NCSEAM)

NCSEAM is funded by the U.S. Department of Education to assist in the implementation of focused monitoring and evidence-based decision-making about compliance with federal law so improved results are achieved for children with disabilities and their families. This Web site features resources on family outcome measurement, downloadable presentations on monitoring priorities and state rank maps.

http://www.monitoringcenter.lsuhsc.edu/

Outcomes 101: ECO Center Q&A's

This page developed by the Early Childhood Outcomes Center summarizes many questions frequently asked about the child and family outcomes measurement process and provides brief answers.

http://www.fpg.unc.edu/~eco/pdfs/ECO_Outcomes101_print_version.pdf

Part C SPP/APR Indicator Analysis

The Regional Resource and Federal Centers (RRFC) Network provides resources on the State Performance Plan (SPP) and the Annual Performance Report (APR). Of particular interest is the analysis of Part C SPP Performance Indicators for all states and territories. The ECO Center provides an analysis of the various approaches states have taken for Indicators 3 and 4, child and family outcomes.

http://www.rrfcnetwork.org/content/view/248/358/

The Power of Outcomes: Strategic Thinking to Improve Results for Our Children, Families, and Communities

In this essay, Cornelius Hogan asserts that programs should employ an outcome and indicator approach that focuses on long-term responsibility and accountability, rather than the traditional activity, productivity, and effectiveness model. He also discusses how programs can improve the well-being of children and families by focusing on outcomes.

http://www.nga.org/Files/pdf/1999OUTCOMES.pdf

Uses and Misuses of Data

Kathleen Hebbeler of the Early Childhood Outcomes Center provides an overview of how outcome data can be used for varying purposes at different levels, including federal, state, local/program, and child/family.

http://www.fpg.unc.edu/~eco/pdfs/ECO_Outcomes_Uses.pdf

Using Outcome Information: Making Data Pay Off

By shifting to an outcome "management" approach (as opposed to outcome "measurement"), programs benefit more from the time-consuming effort of collecting data. The Urban Institute developed this guide to share ways to use outcome information to improve programs and services for young children and families.

http://www.urban.org/UploadedPDF/311040_OutcomeInformation.pdf